Absolute Essentials of International Economics

T0271168

This shortform textbook provides a comprehensive overview of international economics and coverage of recent trends in the global economy to supplement students' knowledge of this fast-moving subject area.

Divided into two parts, the book begins by introducing the fundamental aspects of international economics (the international economic system, global networks and flows, the theory of international trade, trade policy, trade agreements, foreign exchange market, international factor movements, and developing countries) before moving on to focus on specialist topics such as the Covid-19 pandemic, the emerging economies of BRICS, and Brexit. Each chapter includes an essential summary, key terms, study questions, and references.

The book is accompanied by a suite of digital resources, including a test bank of questions, PowerPoints slides, answers to chapter questions, and an instructor's manual.

As part of the Absolute Essentials of Business and Economics series, the book provides a straightforward way for students to learn about international economics, and will be invaluable reading for any student studying the global economy as part of a business, economics or international studies degree programme.

Thomas R. Sadler is Professor of Economics at Western Illinois University. He teaches courses on the Global Economic Environment, Fundamentals of Economic Theory, Environmental Economics, Energy Economics, and the Chicago Economy. His research focuses on environmental policy, energy economics, professional sports leagues, and high-performance organizations.

Absolute Essentials of Business and Economics

Textbooks are an extraordinarily useful tool for students and teachers, as is demonstrated by their continued use in the classroom and online. Successful textbooks run into multiple editions, and in endeavouring to keep up with developments in the field, it can be difficult to avoid increasing length and complexity.

This series of Shortform textbooks offers a range of books which zero-in on the absolute essentials. In focusing on only the core elements of each sub-discipline, the books provide a useful alternative or supplement to traditional textbooks.

Absolute Essentials of Corporate Governance
Stephen Bloomfield

Absolute Essentials of Business Ethics
Peter A. Stanwick & Sarah D. Stanwick

Absolute Essentials of Creative Thinking and Problem Solving
Tony Proctor

Absolute Essentials of Environmental Economics
Barry C. Field

Absolute Essentials of Marketing Research
Bonita M. Kolb

Absolute Essentials of Advertising
Sarah Turnbull

Absolute Essentials of Ethereum
Paul Dylan-Ennis

Absolute Essentials of International Economics
Thomas R. Sadler

For more information about this series, please visit: www.routledge.com/ Absolute-Essentials-of-Business-and-Economics/book-series/ABSOLUTE

Absolute Essentials of International Economics

Thomas R. Sadler

Routledge
Taylor & Francis Group

LONDON AND NEW YORK

First published 2024
by Routledge
4 Park Square, Milton Park, Abingdon, Oxon OX14 4RN

and by Routledge
605 Third Avenue, New York, NY 10158

Routledge is an imprint of the Taylor & Francis Group, an informa business

British Library Cataloguing-in-Publication Data
A catalogue record for this book is available from the
British Library

Library of Congress Cataloguing-in-Publication Data
Names: Sadler, Thomas R., author.
Title: Absolute essentials of international economics /
Thomas R. Sadler.
Description: Abingdon, Oxon ; New York, NY : Routledge, 2024. |
Series: Routledge absolute essentials in business and economics |
Includes bibliographical references and index.
Identifiers: LCCN 2023051115 | ISBN 9781032563152 (hardback) |
ISBN 9781032563084 (paperback) | ISBN 9781003434900 (ebook)
Subjects: LCSH: International economic relations.
Classification: LCC HF1359 .S228 2024 | DDC 337--dc23/eng/
20231121
LC record available at https://lccn.loc.gov/2023051115

ISBN: 978-1-032-56315-2 (hbk)
ISBN: 978-1-032-56308-4 (pbk)
ISBN: 978-1-003-43490-0 (ebk)

DOI: 10.4324/9781003434900

Typeset in Times New Roman
by MPS Limited, Dehradun

Access the Support Material: www.routledge.com/9781032563084

For Holly, Maya, and Mathew with love.

Contents

List of figures	*ix*
List of tables	*xi*
Acknowledgments	*xii*
An overview of the book	*xiii*
Executive summary	*xiv*

1	Introduction to international economics	1

PART I
Fundamentals of international economics   **13**

2	Structure of the global economy	15
3	International trade	24
4	Trade policy	33
5	Trade agreements	44
6	International factor movements	54
7	International monetary system	65
8	Foreign exchange market	74
9	Developing countries and the global economy	85

PART II
Special topics in international economics 97

10 Global economic shock: The coronavirus
    pandemic 99

11 BRICS: The emerging economies of Brazil,
    Russia, India, China, and South Africa 113

12 Brexit: Britain exits the European Union 125

    Index *139*

Figures

1.1	World GDP in constant US dollars	9
1.2	World population in billions	10
2.1	Global networks	19
3.1	United States annual trade deficit (imports – exports) in millions of US dollars	27
4.1	United States trade deficit with China (millions of nominal US dollars)	34
4.2	Export supply curve	35
4.3	Import demand curve	36
4.4	Equilibrium	37
4.5	Consumer surplus	37
4.6	Producer surplus	38
4.7	Effects of a tariff in the importing country	39
4.8	Effects of a subsidy in the exporting country	39
4.9	Effects of an import quota in the importing country	40
4.10	Effects of a voluntary export restraint in the exporting country	41
6.1	Production function	56
6.2	Diminishing marginal product of labor	57
6.3	Labor mobility	58
6.4	Home's economic position	59
6.5	Foreign's economic position	61
8.1	Supply of and demand for dollars in the United Kingdom	80
8.2	Increase in the demand for dollars	81
8.3	Increase in the supply of dollars	82
9.1	Annual global CO_2 emissions in gigatons	88
9.2	Vicious cycle of poverty	95
10.1	Vertical $LRAS$ and long-run equilibrium	101
10.2	Upward-sloping $SRAS$ and short-run equilibrium	102
10.3	Pandemic shock	102
10.4	Negative supply shock	103

10.5   Global supply chain pressure index   106
10.6   Increase in short-run aggregate supply from $SRAS_1$
       to $SRAS_2$ 107
10.7   Change in the consumer price index in the United
       States   109
10.8   Expansionary fiscal policy increases aggregate demand
       from AD_1 to AD_2 109
10.9   Contractionary monetary policy decreases aggregate
       demand from AD_2 to AD 110
11.1   Brazil's GDP per capita in US dollars   117
12.1   Brexit Uncertainty Index, percentage   126
12.2   €/£ exchange rate: number of euros per British pound   130
12.3   Immigration into the United Kingdom in thousands   131
12.4   United Kingdom consumer price inflation, percentage   132
12.5   United Kingdom GDP in chained volume measures,
       seasonally adjusted, £ millions   134
12.6   United Kingdom imports from and exports to the
       EU in current prices, £ millions   135
12.7   United Kingdom unemployment rate, aged 16 and
       over, seasonally adjusted, percentage   136

Tables

1.1	World Bank income classifications	5
1.2	Number of countries by World Bank income classification in 2023	6
3.1	Level of trade for selected countries in 2020	26
8.1	Rate of return in dollars and pounds	80
9.1	Examples of developing countries	86
9.2	Countries with the highest Gini coefficients	92
10.1	Unemployment rates in the European Union and United States in 2020	105
11.1	Income classifications and GDP	114
11.2	World's top oil producers in 2022	118

Acknowledgments

I thank Routledge for publishing this book. At every step of the writing process, Chloe Herbert and Michelle Gallagher provided helpful feedback and encouragement. It has been a pleasure working with them.

Professionally, I benefit from the interaction with many colleagues, including Tara Feld, Jessica Lin, Manda Tiwari, Aastha Gupta, Shankar Ghimire, Jobu Babin, Braxton Gately, Alla Melkumian, and Haritima Chauhan. Thank you for our ongoing conversations about economics and life. I thank the WIU Foundation and Office of Sponsored Projects for helpful funding with this project.

Personally, I enjoy the support from a wonderful family, including Judy, Charles, Laura, Chris, Mark, Fred, and Rick.

I dedicate this book and all of my work to Holly, Maya, and Mathew. I love you very much.

Thomas R. Sadler

An Overview of the Book

The book includes two parts. Chapter 1 introduces the topic of international economics. Part I addresses the fundamentals of international economics, including the structure of the global economy (chapter 2), international trade (chapter 3), trade policy (chapter 4), trade agreements (chapter 5), international factor movements (chapter 6), international monetary system (chapter 7), foreign exchange market (chapter 8), and developing countries and the global economy (chapter 9). Part II considers special topics in international economics, including the coronavirus pandemic as a global economic shock (chapter 10), the emerging BRICS economies (chapter 11), and the economic implications of Brexit (chapter 12). In Part II, instructors interested in specific topics may cover the chapters in any order.

Executive Summary

Each chapter begins with an executive summary, which provides a brief review of the chapter's material. Students using the book are encouraged to read the executive summary before beginning each chapter and then returning to it upon completion.

1 Introduction to international economics

ESSENTIAL SUMMARY

Globalization, the growing level of interconnection between countries, companies, and individuals, serves as the driving force for global economic change. Current global economic trends stem from world events that occurred in the 1990s, including the fall of the Soviet Union. The World Bank designates the economies of the world by four income groups: high, upper-middle, lower-middle, and low income. The study of international economics uses the same tools as other areas in the field of economics, including economic models. An analysis of the global economy demonstrates that most production stems from privately owned means of production in decentralized markets. Three factors contribute to the process of economic growth: accumulation of capital stock, increases in economic resource inputs such as labor, and technological advances.

Uneven effects

The economic forces that characterize the modern age, including international trade, expanding markets, networks of exchange, and global supply chains, have led to prosperity for many, but not all, of the world's inhabitants. **Globalization**, the growing level of interconnection between countries, companies, and individuals, serves as the driving force for these processes. It liberalizes trade, maximizes efficiency, and opens markets. As globalization occurs, rising income levels accompany economic growth. Other benefits exist. Consumers enjoy imports from countries around the world. Advances in innovation and technology increase the world's level of interconnection. Expanding access to goods and services, investment, and economic systems leads to

DOI: 10.4324/9781003434900-1

higher living standards. For many of the world's citizens, globalization has led to higher levels of prosperity. But problems persist.

Import competition leads to losses in manufacturing jobs. As countries such as China, India, and Mexico ramp up their manufacturing sectors and export goods to the rest of the world, displaced factory workers experience falling wages and decreasing employment opportunities. Often public support systems are insufficient in their abilities to compensate individuals for these losses. Many workers without transferable skills, especially in manufacturing, suffer permanent losses in income. Regions where job losses occur experience economic decline.

In the early 2020s, several global disruptions occurred. During the coronavirus pandemic, the movement to integrate global markets and decrease production costs reduced the number of face masks and medical gloves for health care workers, semiconductors for automobile manufacturers, and retail items for consumers. Increasing economic integration, trade, and the flow of information could not prevent the conflict between Russia and Ukraine. Extreme weather events from climate change such as rising temperatures and drought disrupted power systems, destroyed crops, and increased the number of climate refugees crossing country borders.

The point is that globalization – a force expanding around the world – evolves over time, leading to uneven outcomes. During this century, the United States has experienced a growing level of economic integration with the rest of the world. But the number of domestic manufacturing jobs has declined. At the same time, other non-farm forms of employment have increased. The result is a decrease in the country's share of employment from manufacturing as a percentage of total employment (Fort et al., 2018). Even though the US economy normally creates jobs on an annual basis, and many of these jobs in services and technology are connected to global markets, most of the jobs are created outside of the manufacturing sector.

Countries, companies, and individuals are linked through global networks of finance, production, and trade. In the United States, both exports and imports have risen every decade since the 1970s. But imports have grown faster, creating a trade deficit. The United States pays for this deficit with an inflow of financial capital, the foreign purchases of domestic securities such as Treasury debt, U.S. corporate bonds, and stocks. The funding for the inflow of capital comes from central banks, foreign corporations, global hedge funds, and sovereign wealth funds. But the foreign financial investment drives up the value of the US dollar, which weakens domestic agricultural producers and the manufacturing base.

This book on the *Absolute Essentials of International Economics* argues that the process of globalization generates income and wealth, creates conditions for economic growth, and leads to technological advances; however, not everyone benefits from this process. As a result, the study of international economics is important because it analyzes why some economic agents benefit from the international flow of goods, services, and money, but some don't.

The global economy that has resulted from a growing level of interconnection exhibits ongoing areas of turbulence, exemplified by the disruptions from financial crises, the pandemic, regional conflict, and climate change. It is therefore important to study the conditions that characterize the global economy. To put these topics in perspective, the remainder of the chapter discusses global economic trends, World Bank income classifications, the study of international economics, and the future of the global economy. The chapter concludes with a section on how to use this book.

Global economic trends

Global economic trends stem from world events that began in the 1990s. Following the collapse of the Soviet Union in December 1991, the theorist Francis Fukuyama declared that the fall of communism marked the "end of history," meaning that free market capitalism won the twentieth-century cold war battle (Fukuyama, 1992). Free markets and liberal democratic values not only established better social systems, according to Fukuyama, but served as "the end point of mankind's ideological evolution." During the 1990s and into the twenty-first century, the growth of capitalism on a global scale seemed inevitable.

The belief was that growing levels of prosperity were a function of free markets, laissez-faire government, and profit maximization. At the same time, higher levels of economic integration and the establishment of global networks of exchange would end both conflicts between countries and undemocratic forms of government. Over time, economic growth would benefit countries, companies, and individuals.

Positive economic trends

During the 1990s and the first two and a half decades of this century, global production rose at a steady rate, the only downturns occurring during the financial crisis of 2008–2009 and the coronavirus pandemic of 2020–2022. At the same time, inflation remained in check, while employment, productivity, and wages increased. The global exchange of goods and services, as measured by exports and imports, demonstrated the importance of regional trade agreements and the ability of companies to contribute to global supply chains. Investment in global markets, including those in lower-income countries, persisted. Most of the major global stock markets showed steady gains.

In 2001, China's entry into the World Trade Organization – which establishes the rule of trade between nations – served as a transformative event, linking China's markets with more than 100 other countries around the world. The rural residents in China who moved into cities in a process of urbanization provided their labor services to the manufacturing sector, which lifted hundreds of millions of individuals out of poverty. This change contributed to sectoral growth in China's economy, including computers, furniture, vehicles, toys, games, clothing, and accessories. Most of these goods were exported to the rest of the world.

Ongoing problems

While economic growth, rising incomes, and an increase in employment serve as global economic successes since 1991, the process of globalization has also led to ongoing problems. Deepening inequalities, environmental degradation, and the climate crisis serve as three examples. Exporting jobs from higher-income countries such as the United States to lower-income countries exists as another.

Policy makers knew that globalization possessed both benefits and costs. But when markets were left to answer questions concerning the deployment of workers, resource allocation, and technological advances, the objective of profit maximization often trumped the ideas of environmental and social responsibility. The desire to find low-wage workers enhanced the potential for labor exploitation. Higher levels of global exchange increased the flow of pollution. A focus on the production and distribution of cars, cell phones, and t-shirts minimized the need for education, health care, and housing. In higher-income countries, the exodus of manufacturing jobs decreased wages and the bargaining power of workers, creating anti-immigrant sentiment and populist movements. Many countries struggled to reapportion the benefits and costs of globalization.

In 2020, when the coronavirus pandemic spread worldwide in a process of contagion, all countries suffered from rising death tolls, increasing levels of morbidity, and economic losses. But, in many poorer countries, the conditions were dire. Soaring prices for food caused by global shortages and the war in Ukraine wreaked havoc on household budgets. Country-level debts, which were often denominated in dollars, increased when interest rates rose in the United States. As became clear in the 2020s, markets, on their own, would not automatically allocate economic resources productively, enhance democratic processes, establish environmental standards, or redistribute income in an equitable manner.

The global economic environment

While the collapse of the Soviet Union gave way to the rise of free-market orthodoxy in the 1990s, the coronavirus pandemic, war in Ukraine, inflation, insecure supply chains, and climate crisis in the 2020s demonstrated the need for a balanced approach to global prosperity. As this book explains, global institutions such as the World Bank oversee expanding trade networks. Regional trade agreements establish the rules of exchange, which enhance the ability of countries to supply goods and services to the rest of the world. International factor movements and direct foreign investment enhance the productive capacity of domestic economies. The international monetary system ensures the flow of money in financial markets. While global economic networks create imbalances between countries, and many flaws exist, the process of globalization serves as the dominant economic force in the world today. The path to prosperity, in other words, entails economic tradeoffs.

World Bank income classifications

In international economics, the World Bank establishes an important method of classification. The World Bank designates economies as high, upper-middle, lower-middle, or low income. Based on **Gross National Income** (GNI), the total amount of income earned by a country's businesses and individuals annually, the World Bank updates the classifications on July 1 of each year, according to GNI from the previous year. The GNI measures are denominated in US dollars, establishing a common metric. For two reasons, country classifications may change. First, economic growth, exchange rate fluctuation, employment, inflation, and population growth alter GNI. Second, the World Bank changes the classification thresholds on an annual basis, in order to keep the country categories fixed in real terms. Table 1.1 provides the income classifications for 2022 and 2023.

Table 1.1 World Bank income classifications

Group	2023	2022
Low income	<$1,085	<$1,045
Lower-middle income	$1,086–$4,255	$1,046–$4,095
Upper-middle income	$4,256–$13,205	$4,096–$12,695
High income	>$13,205	>$12,695

Source: World Bank, https://blogs.worldbank.org/opendata/new-world-bank-country-classifications-income-level-2022-2023.

Table 1.2 Number of countries by World Bank income classification in 2023

Group	Number of countries	Status
Low income	26	Developing
Lower-middle income	54	Developing
Upper-middle income	54	Developing
High income	83	Developed

Source: World Bank, https://datahelpdesk.worldbank.org/knowledgebase/articles/906519-world-bank-country-and-lending-groups.

In analyzing the income classifications, several observations exist. First, a country is considered a **developing country** if it has an income classification below the high-income level. A country is considered a **developed country** if it has high-income status. In 2023, although 83 countries were considered developed, 134 were classified as developing (Table 1.2). Second, on an annual basis, little movement exists between income classifications. It is difficult, in other words, for a country to move up on the list.

The reason it is difficult for countries to move up on the list is the challenge of economic development. This process entails an improvement in the living standards of all of a country's inhabitants. But it also requires overcoming inefficient governments, a lack of investment in education and training, and the challenge of strengthening markets. Often countries with lower income levels struggle to achieve these objectives. According to the World Bank, between 2022 and 2023, little movement existed between income categories. Belize moved from lower-middle income to upper-middle income. Panama and Romania moved from upper-middle income to high income. But countries also moved in the opposite direction. Lebanon moved from upper-middle income to lower-middle income. Palau moved from high income to upper-middle income. Zambia moved from lower-middle income to low income. For these countries, both economic problems and conflict worsened economic conditions.

The study of international economics

The study of international economics uses the same tools as other areas in the field of economics, including economic models. Supply and demand models of import demand and export supply, along with trade policies, provide a framework to analyze trade flows. A model of production possibilities establishes context for international factor movements. A supply and demand model of foreign exchange analyzes currency fluctuations. The aggregate demand and aggregate supply model shows how the coronavirus pandemic devasted economies. The point is that, in international economics, models provide a framework to address economic activity.

Structure of the global economy

Chapter 2 explains that the global economy includes exchange, interconnected functions, and material operations. In a dynamic environment, these processes increase during periods of prosperity and decrease during periods of contraction. The global economy includes macro structures (global institutions, trade agreements, and organizations), global networks (processes that create connections between economic agents), and uneven outcomes (conflict, instability, and an inequitable distribution of income). Together, these factors create a growing level of income, output, and wealth for countries, companies, and individuals, but also inequitable outcomes for the economic agents who do not benefit from the existing order.

Gains from trade, policy, and trade agreements

Chapters 3–5 discuss international trade, policy, and agreements, arguing that the potential gains from trade – when countries export and import goods and services with each other – motivate international production decisions. The reality, however, is that the international economy establishes a large range of circumstances in which trade is beneficial. Trade between two countries may create mutual benefits even if one country is more technologically advanced than the other. Mutually beneficial trade places countries in position to produce and export output with lower domestic opportunity costs. Regional trade agreements increase the level of integration of member countries. But restrictive trade policy protects domestic industries or punishes trading partners. It also increases consumer prices, decreases production, and leads to efficiency losses.

Factor movements

Chapter 6 argues that international factor movements enable markets to adjust to changing economic conditions. International factor movements involve the exchange of economic resource inputs, including capital and labor. While labor mobility occurs less frequently than capital mobility, labor mobility exists as a way to address labor market imbalances. For example, if a region experiences economic growth and a shortage of labor, workers move to the region, reducing the labor market shortage. In addition to international factor movements, investment by economic agents in foreign countries enhances the potential for economic growth. The reason is that foreign investment leads to the transfer of human capital and accumulation of physical capital. This transfer increases the productivity of economic resources.

International monetary system and foreign exchange

Chapters 7–8 discuss the international monetary system and market for foreign exchange. An exchange rate is the price of one currency in terms of another. The global monetary system is characterized by floating exchange rates, when currency values are determined by the forces of supply and demand. In this system, the market alters currency values, not government controls or trade restrictions. Market equilibrium occurs when an exchange rate equates the quantity of currency demanded with the quantity of currency supplied. When economic shocks impact economies, however, exchange rate volatility occurs, increasing market risk. The history of the international monetary system includes the gold standard, fixed exchange rate system, and beginning of the current era.

Developing countries

Chapter 9 discusses developing countries and the global economy. Developing countries are diverse with respect to their economies and social conditions. They may have access to large foreign markets, but experience lower levels of economic efficiency and productivity. Low-income countries struggle to establish the conditions necessary for economic development. Ongoing problems include a lack of effective governance, low levels of investment in education and training, and inefficient markets. While middle-income economies possess better infrastructures and governance than their low-income counterparts, they may struggle with conflict, inequality, and poverty. But developing countries share with developed countries the objectives of establishing stronger economies and a greater access to education, healthcare, and housing.

Special topics

Chapters 10–12 discuss special topics. Chapter 10 addresses the global economic effects of the coronavirus pandemic. The pandemic existed as an economic shock, an unexpected and large-scale event that disrupted economic activity. The pandemic led to a decrease in production, increase in unemployment, and disruption of global supply chains. Chapter 11 considers the emerging economies of Brazil, Russia, India, China, and South Africa. These countries play an important role in international economies, providing both output and resources to the rest of the world. Chapter 12 explains that Britain's decision to exit the European Union (Brexit) serves as the largest reversal of economic integration in the modern era. The economic effects of the decision were mixed. While an inflow of immigration, inflation, production, and imports increased after Brexit, the value of the pound and level of employment remained stable.

The future of the global economy

The study of international economics demonstrates that most economic growth stems from privately owned means of production in decentralized markets. According to the World Bank, world GDP as measured in current US dollars increased from $1.38 trillion in 1960 to $22.86 trillion in 1990 to $85.22 trillion in 2020 (Figure 1.1).

Three factors contribute to the process of economic growth: accumulation of capital stock, increase in economic resource inputs such as labor, and technological advance. In the long term, technological advance serves as the main driver of economic growth. In the short term, the accumulation of capital stock progresses at a steady rate. On a global scale, the population continues to increase (Figure 1.2). In developed countries such as the United States and the United

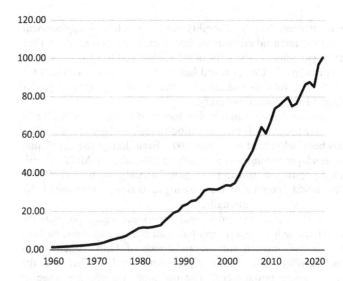

Figure 1.1 World GDP in constant US dollars.

Source: Author using data from the World Bank, https://data.worldbank.org/indicator/NY.GDP.MKTP.CD?end=2022&start=1960&view=chart.

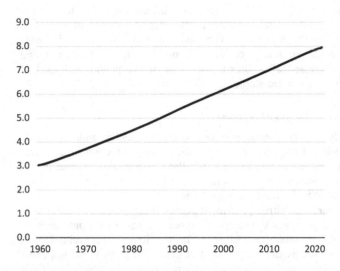

Figure 1.2 World population in billions.

Source: Author using data from the World Bank, https://data.worldbank.org/indicator/SP.POP.TOTL.

Kingdom, however, the rate of fertility has fallen below the replacement level. While the financial crisis in the first decade of this century and the coronavirus pandemic in the third decade influenced this trend, population growth in the developed world has been on a downward trend for many years. The reasons include economic prosperity, greater gender equality, and lower infant mortality.

Demographers estimate that, in the absence of immigration, 2.1 births per woman are necessary for a population to replenish itself. The United States has been below that level since 2007. Even though the population of many developing countries, especially in sub-Saharan Africa, experience higher population growth rates, global fertility has been declining. In fact, the world's population is increasing at its slowest rate since 1950, falling below one percent annually.

Much of the developed world will experience aging populations. While countries such as Nigeria and Pakistan continue to grow, parts of Central Asia and Eastern Europe and much of Latin America will experience fertility rates below replacement levels. What are the outcomes of aging populations? The outcomes include a change in global migration patterns, limits on the prospects for economic growth, new capital flows and investment patterns, the need for new social safety nets, and the slowing of the process of urbanization.

The United Nations forecasts that world population will peak at around 10.8 billion people in the 2080s before declining after 2100. In economic terms, two areas of concern exist. First, older populations with fewer children send a lower percentage of workers into the labor force. Second, older populations leave fewer working-age adults to support a country's retirees. Together, these factors demonstrate challenging conditions for the global labor force.

The system of global capitalism has major flaws, including an inequitable distribution of income, the negative externalities of climate change and pollution, and a tendency to succumb to global shocks such as financial crises and pandemics. But the global economy allocates economic resources, expands access to markets, and establishes incentives for innovation. Capitalism aligns systematic and individual objectives, including the desire to improve human living standards. The problem is that economic conditions change in uneven ways. Developing countries may struggle to improve their low-income status. Individuals living at the margin of society may not be able to access the formal markets. Companies may not adapt to changing economic circumstances. The study of international economics addresses these issues, establishing a framework of analysis for global economic problems and solutions.

How to use this book

This book discusses international economics. It covers the important areas of the subject, including the structure of the global economy, international trade, international factor movements, international monetary system, foreign exchange market, and developing economies. Instructors may use the book as a stand-alone or supplemental text. It is a useful book for undergraduate courses on international economics or the global economic environment. The book is also helpful for business or social science students interested in learning about international economics, but do not want to enroll in a course or read a standard textbook. The book is useful for learning about current issues such as the economic effects of the coronavirus pandemic, emerging economies, and Brexit. While it is helpful to cover the chapters in order in Part 1, instructors interested in special topics may cover the chapters in Part 2 in any order.

Key terms

Developed country
Developing country
Globalization
Gross National Income

Questions

1 Does everyone benefit from the process of globalization? Why or why not?
2 Have previous events helped to establish the contemporary global economic environment? Explain and provide specific examples.
3 For the study of international economics, what economic tools are important?
4 What is the significance of World Bank income classifications?
5 Over time, what factors influence the process of economic growth?

References

Fort, Teresa, Pierce, Justin and Schott, Peter. 2018. "New Perspectives on the Decline of US Manufacturing Employment." *Journal of Economic Perspectives*, 32(2): 47–72.

Fukuyama, Francis. 1992. *The End of History and the Last Man.* Glencoe: Free Press.

Part I

Fundamentals of international economics

2 Structure of the global economy

ESSENTIAL SUMMARY

The novel coronavirus spread through a system of interconnection –
a network – which is a group of informed parts that are linked
together. The global economy exists in a broad relational framework with exchange, interconnected functions, and material operations. Global networks – including financial, migration, production,
social, technology, and trade – are important elements of the international economy. Even though the process of globalization
increases the flow of goods and services, expands markets, and
increases income, it also leads to uneven outcomes.

Coronavirus pandemic and human transmission

In early 2020, the novel coronavirus spread through a system of
interconnection – a human transmission **network**. An integrated network
is characterized by a group of informed parts that are linked together. In
the case of the novel coronavirus, the informed parts were individuals
throughout the world. When we think of networks, we often focus on the
social networks that connect individuals or the trade networks that
connect countries. On the whole, these networks create net benefits for
society. But the spread of the infectious pathogen that led to the global
pandemic occurred in a network of contagion. The carriers of the novel
coronavirus in one region infected people in other regions. After the
initial outbreak, many countries that closed their borders slowed down
human transmission, but could not eliminate the spread of the virus. The
lesson from the millions of global cases and deaths during the pandemic
is that it is difficult to stop an infectious virus from spreading around the
world. In the context of the global economy, once networks are created,
they facilitate both positive and negative flows.

DOI: 10.4324/9781003434900-3

Structure of the global economy

The global economy is characterized by a growing level of inter-connection between countries, companies, and individuals. **Value chains** – the economic activities that lead to the delivery of a valuable economic resource input or form of output to an end customer – include several global trends. First, international trade is becoming less goods-intensive. That is, while production continues to increase, a smaller share of the goods produced at the country level flows across borders. Second, cross-border services are increasing at a faster rate than the trade in goods. Third, the trade in goods is less likely to entail labor-cost advantages. More often, it relies on production infrastructure and economies of scale. Fourth, with respect to the labor that is involved in international trade, value chains are relying more on high-skilled labor. Finally, value chains are becoming more concentrated at the regional level, for example, within Asia, Europe, and North America (Lund et al., 2019).

The global economy exists in a broad relational framework with exchange, interconnected functions, and material operations. The processes and relationships exist in a dynamic environment, expanding with favorable market conditions and contracting during periods of global instability, pandemic, or war. The global economy includes macro-structures, networks of interaction, and uneven outcomes.

Macro structures

Macro structures include material practices, such as institutions, trade agreements, interconnections, and organizations. Global institutions facilitate international exchange, establish the rules of interaction, and provide aid to countries. For international trade, rules and regulations are set at the global level. Global institutions facilitate the processes of economic growth, exchange, and oversight. They help to solve currency problems. They attempt to level the economic playing field. Three major global economic institutions exist: International Monetary Fund (IMF), World Bank, and World Trade Organization (WTO).

Global institutions

The IMF supports economic policies that achieve financial stability, monetary cooperation, and sustainable growth. A global institution established in 1944 during the World War II era, the IMF provides loans to member countries to address balance of payments problems, monitors the international monetary system to minimize risks, and provides technical assistance and training to central banks and governments in areas such as climate change, corruption, gender equality, and income inequality.

The World Bank works for sustainable solutions for poverty reduction and shared prosperity. A goal of the World Bank is to decrease extreme poverty at the global level from 10 percent to 3 percent. Another goal is to increase the incomes of the poorest 40 percent of the global population. As a source of funding and information, the World Bank serves as the major global institution for developing economies.

The WTO establishes the rules of trade between nations, using trade as a method to increase living standards. WTO agreements between countries – negotiated and signed by trading partners – are ratified in individual parliaments. The agreements establish a framework for trade in a free, predictable, and reliable manner. By overseeing trade flows, the WTO helps countries increase their potential output, while providing a mechanism to address trade disputes.

Interconnections

In the global economy, many economic flows exist, because porosity characterizes national borders. Monetary flows involve central banks, commercial banks, and individuals. Trade flows that include cell phones, vehicles, and many other forms of output are multi-directional: economic resource inputs originate in different countries. Pollution creates reverse flows when developed countries outsource polluting industries to developing countries and then experience lower air quality. Positive flows such as finance, technology, and trade increase human well-being (Ritzer and Dean, 2021).

Negative flows include air pollution, borderless diseases, crime, dangerous imports, terrorism, and war. These flows alter human societies, increasing their level of vulnerability, the state of being exposed to harm (Ritzer and Dean, 2021). In some cases, such as global pandemics and war, a large number of people may become sick or die. In other cases, such as crime or dangerous imports, insecurity rises for members of a population. With negative flows, the development of globalization and the Internet means individuals may disseminate alternative perspectives through social media. Fake news and inaccurate information serve as examples, occurring during the coronavirus pandemic and the war in Ukraine.

Choke points and **regulatory mechanisms** are important. Choke points are strategic passages that connect different areas of the world. The Strait of Hormuz, connecting the Persian Gulf and the Gulf of Oman, exists as one of the world's most important choke points because of its key role in the flow of oil. When political turmoil complicates economic conditions, this choke point may reduce the flow of oil out of the region. With the flow of migrants, regulatory mechanisms may either simplify or complicate the ability of individuals to enter a country.

Important examples include policies regulating migrants entering the European Union or the United States. Migrants are often willing to take undesirable forms of employment, work longer hours, and receive lower salaries. But migrants also contribute diversity to an economy.

Structures and organizations

While economic resources and output flow in global networks, certain structures and organizations create friction, including corporations, countries, and labor unions. The process of globalization increases the world's level of openness; however, it also blocks certain channels of movement. One example is the toughening of border controls because of a hostility toward refugees and undocumented immigrants. A second example is a trade agreement that facilitates the flow of output but restricts the flow of labor. A third example is when a country blocks economic transactions that it views as detrimental to the national interest, such as military output to suspect countries. A final example is when labor unions oppose the flow of undocumented immigrants because they are willing to work for lower wages. Even in the presence of these forms of friction, it is difficult to stop the flow of illegal goods. Countries cannot inspect all imports. But it is easier to erect barriers that reduce or stop the flow of tangible forms of output than it is to stop the flow of information and technology (Ritzer and Dean, 2021).

Trade agreements

Trade agreements between countries in the Europe, North America, and other regions encourage economic integration. But policies such as tariffs (taxes on imports) reduce trade flows. In the European Union, the majority of imports entering the region experience a zero-tariff rate, but tariffs often exist on some consumer goods. In the United States, the ports of Los Angeles, Long Beach, and New Jersey/New York – the three biggest in the country – facilitate shipping. When operating efficiently, these ports enhance trade flows. In general, pathways that expedite trade include intercontinental airline routes, paths of migration, global value chains, and points of entry.

Global networks

The process of globalization creates new relationships between economic agents. Networks serve as facilitators. First, networks facilitate the flow of goods, services, money, and economic resources. Second, they create an ever-expanding web of linkages. Third, they exist at different scales. Many useful examples exist.

Global networks such as fiber optic cables connect countries, increasing the flow of information. International production networks enhance the ability of companies to produce output. Larger networks such as these form economic clusters, serving as defining characteristics of the global economy. But smaller networks also exist. National networks of exchange are bounded by country borders. Regional and local networks exist at the sub-national level. These smaller networks help to connect companies and individuals.

In a network, a **node** is a point in which a pathway intersects or branches out. In a social network, individuals serve as nodes. In trade networks, companies serve as nodes. In financial networks, banks serve as nodes. Nodes are important because they increase both the size of the network and degree of interconnection. On a global scale, nodes facilitate liquid flows, meaning the things that move easily from one place to another. One example is the information that flows between computers. Another example is the food that flows between distributors, including bananas from Ecuador, rice from India, and sushi from Japan. Because networks exist in all sizes, it is now easier to communicate, exchange goods and services, seek information, and establish global markets. Even though networks exist in all scales, the following sections focus on global networks that are important in international economics (Figure 2.1).

Figure 2.1 Global networks.
Source: Author.

Finance

The global financial network facilitates exchange between borrowers and lenders, manages liquidity, and transfers risk between economic agents. But the financial network experiences the risk of contagion, the spreading of a harmful outcomes between nodes. An example is the global financial crisis 2008–2009. First, financial markets may experience friction that interferes with exchange. Second, financial crises are nonlinear events with sharp decreases in asset prices. The financial crisis was characterized by a buildup of vulnerabilities, including a housing boom, rising mortgage debt, relaxation of lending standards, and speculation about future price increases in the housing market. These factors increased the level of vulnerability of both banks and households. When housing prices fell, over-lending by banks and mortgage defaults weakened economic activity. The result was a collapse of some investment banks and the spreading of risk to financial institutions, households, and nonfinancial firms. Aggressive measures of intervention by the US Federal Reserve System prevented a collapse of the global economy (Gertler and Gilchrist, 2018).

Migration

Migrants cross country borders. Some move for economic opportunity. But others flee conflicts or climatic changes, including droughts, earthquakes, famine, and floods. Because individuals may leave for positive or negative reasons, a global network of migration exists. Empirically, hundreds of millions of people migrate on an annual basis. One outcome is that individuals who move send remittances back to their home countries, worth hundreds of billions of dollars each year. A second outcome is richer countries attract migrants, especially from developing countries with younger populations. A third outcome is that many migrants exist as climate refugees. As the world becomes warmer, the movement of individuals from one region to others results from environmental instability. As a result, climatic changes exist as threats to civilization as they grow in intensity and frequency. Overall, international migration is a function of demographic, economic, environmental, and geographic factors.

Production

Global production networks include the interconnected processes, methods, and forms of exchange through which goods and services are produced, distributed, and consumed. These networks have several characteristics, including their geography, dynamic nature, and tendency to adjust. They exist as economic phenomena with organizational fields, economic agents, and governance. The global production network for cell phones, for example, includes raw material extraction, component manufacture, assembly, distribution, consumption, and disposal. Each stage is embedded in non-linear sets of relationships. The steps are interconnected, each serving as an important element of the process. The raw materials in cell phones depend on the brand, but common materials include silicon, plastic, iron, aluminum, copper, lead, zinc, tin, and nickel, which are mined or manufactured around the world. At its core, global production networks have interconnected nodes and links that cross national boundaries, creating value through the transformation of economic resource inputs into different forms of output. They exist in the environment in which they are grounded. As a result, global production networks are processes of material transformation and subject to environmental changes, the organization of energy and matter, and the markets in which they exist (Coe et al., 2008).

Social

Social networks depict the connections between individuals, social units, or organizations. These networks facilitate business connections, communication, and the flow of information. Examples include hospitals in a network, computer programmers in a system of outsourcing, designers working for multinational corporations, or skeptics in the public realm. The nature of the relationships between agents, size of the network, and functionality of the linkages establish network structure, which may encompass a group of friends in a community, businesses in an industry, or agents in global institutions. As social networks have proliferated, they offer many benefits, including connections, support, and technology. The problem is that social networks may also exist as conduits for epistemic oppression, when exclusion from truthful pronouncements reduces or prohibits an individual's ability to contribute to knowledge production. These mechanisms establish relationships between individuals, structures, and outcomes. Networks demonstrate the multidimensional nature of participating agents.

Technology

The development of both products and markets is a function of the advancement of science and technology. In a world of globalization, scientific progress and technological advance bring new ideas, methods, and forms of output to the global economy. But scientific research and technological innovation develop in tandem. When scientific progress creates new ways to turn economic resource inputs into output, global networks of technology develop. This process establishes opportunities in multiple sectors, including artificial intelligence, biotechnology, electric vehicles, renewable energy, and semiconductors. A connection exists between scientists, inventors, and entrepreneurs, the individuals who act as gatekeepers in their fields. They bridge the gap between science, technology, and economics. As globalization increases, global networks of technology expand. The implication of the co-evolution of science and technology is that governments around the world establish methods to encourage scientific advance and the transfer of technology from laboratories and universities to the private sector. The idea is to support both entrepreneurs and scientists through incentives and intellectual property rights (Breschi and Catalini, 2010).

Trade

International trade – the flow of output from exporting countries to their importing destinations – exists in a global network. As the global economy expanded, the international trade network increased. Goods and services find global markets, increasing the ability of economic resource inputs to participate in the process of globalization. The economic analysis of individual sectors, such as consulting, electronics, or tourism, provides the opportunity to attach a value to the strength of individual trade flows. Tourism, for example, expands over time as a share of the global economy unless it is disrupted by a global shock. The point is that studying the global network of trade describes network structure, the pattern of trade flows, and role of countries. Global trade is characterized by several trends, including a higher share of trade in economic resource inputs, growing level of interconnection between countries and companies, and an increasing role for emerging economies. As the global network of trade changes and number of links between nodes rises, the value of international trade increases (De Benedictis and Tajoli, 2011).

Uneven outcomes

Even though the process of globalization increases the flow of goods and services, expands markets, and increases global incomes, it also leads to uneven outcomes, including conflict, instability, and an inequitable distribution of income. Globalization creates a greater level of interconnection; however, in many contexts, it benefits privileged countries and individuals at the expense of the countries and individuals at the other end of the spectrum. One way to view this reality is to envision the world in terms of the core and periphery, where the core consists of the wealthy and powerful countries that establish the world order. The periphery consists of the developing countries that struggle to share in the benefits of globalization. Uneven outcomes take the form of class inequality, race/ethnic/gender inequality, urban-rural inequality, and the North/South divide. The outcomes include conflict traps with continuing civil wars, a global digital divide, inefficient governance, and economic problems in low-income countries. In the end, uneven outcomes may decrease productivity, increase disparities in human health, and limit opportunities for those with lower income levels.

Key terms

Choke points
Network
Node
Regulatory mechanisms
Value chains

Questions

1 Why is a network important in considering the spread of the novel coronavirus?
2 What elements contribute to the structure of the global economy? Explain each element.
3 How do macro structures help to characterize the global economy?
4 List and describe the global networks in this chapter. Why are the networks important for the understanding of international economics?
5 Why does the global economy lead to uneven outcomes?

References

Breschi, Stefano and Catalini, Christian. 2010. "Tracing the Links between Science and Technology: An Exploratory Analysis of Scientists' and Inventors' Networks." *Research Policy*, 39(1): 14–26.

Coe, Neil, Dicken, Peter and Hess, Martin. 2008. "Global Production Networks: Realizing the Potential." *Journal of Economic Geography*, 8(3): 271–295.

De Benedictis, Luca and Tajoli, Lucia. 2011. "The World Trade Network." *The World Economy*, 34(8): 1417–1454.

Gertler, Mark and Gilchrist, Simon. 2018. "What Happened: Financial Factors in the Great Recession." *Journal of Economic Perspectives*, 32(3): 3–30.

Lund, Susan, Manyika, James, Woetzel, Jonathan, Bughin, Jacques, Krishnan, Mekala, Seong, Jeongmin and Muir, Mac. 2019. *Globalization in Transition: The Future of Trade and Value Chains*. Washington, DC: McKinsey Global Institute.

Ritzer, George and Dean, Paul. 2021. *Globalization: A Basic Text*, 3rd Edition. Oxford: Wiley-Blackwell.

3 International trade

ESSENTIAL SUMMARY

As a global shock, the coronavirus pandemic, in addition to ravaging human health and reducing world output, disrupted global trade. A country's level of trade refers to its exports as a percentage of GDP. A country's balance of trade measures the difference between the monetary value of its exports and imports over a period of time. Sources of the gains from international trade include comparative advantage, market expansion, price reduction, and a variety of products. Distributional consequences of international trade exist in the form of effects on consumption, the labor market, and poverty. The arguments against free trade include countering foreign subsidies and dumping, the infant industry argument, and protecting domestic jobs.

The pandemic and trade disruption

Between 2020 and 2022, the coronavirus pandemic, in addition to ravaging human health and reducing world production, disrupted global trade. Because governments issued household lockdowns and economic shutdowns to contain the spread of the pathogen, manufacturing declined, the volume of container shipping decreased, supply chains shuttered, and distribution systems were disrupted. Before the onset of the coronavirus pandemic, **global production networks** – the interconnected operations and transactions in which goods and services are produced, distributed, and consumed – spanned the entire globe, benefitting both developed and developing countries, promoting globalization, and increasing productivity.

The pandemic reduced the scope of global production networks. The gap narrowed between the origin of production in countries such as

DOI: 10.4324/9781003434900-4

China, India, and South Korea and the points of consumption (Vidya and Prabheesh, 2020). In effect, the pandemic, as a negative supply shock, distorted global production networks. The reasons included lower levels of labor force participation, problems with global shipping, and disruptions in national and regional transportation systems. While global trade expanded after 2022, the pandemic served as a lesson in how a global supply shock may ravage global production networks.

During the coronavirus pandemic, several factors contributed to a reduction in international trade. First, governments implemented travel restrictions such as border closings, household quarantines, and social distancing. Second, transportation and travel costs increased, including the costs of freight, economic resource inputs, and shipping time. Third, the interruption of air transportation reduced global passenger traffic and commercial air cargo. Fourth, the pandemic reduced business travel and face-to-face meetings. Fifth, policy instability existed with trade restrictions, regulatory differences, and cross-border transportation costs. Together, these measures reduced economic activity in trade, tourism, and related industries, highlighting the importance of international exchange in national economies (Vo and Tran, 2021).

Trade flows

Countries, companies, and individuals conduct business with each other because they expect to experience economic gains. In previous centuries, traders on the Silk Road – a network of routes between Asia and Europe that was used for more than 1,500 years – brought silk, spices, tea, and other goods from Asia while glassware, precious metals, textiles, and other goods came from Europe. Today, most countries have **open economies**, actively engaging in international trade. Few examples exist of **closed economies**, when countries do not trade with the rest of the world.

A difference exists between a country's **level of trade** and its **balance of trade**. A country's level of trade – measured as exports as a percentage of GDP – is determined by geographic location, productivity of export industries, size of the economy, and trade history. A higher level of trade means a country exports a larger percentage of its production compared to other countries. According to the World Bank, in 2020, world exports as a percentage of global GDP equaled 26 percent. At the country level, China's level of trade equaled 20 percent, India's equaled 21 percent, the United Kingdom's equaled 28 percent, and the United States' equaled 11 percent (Table 3.1).

A country's balance of trade measures the difference between the monetary value of its exports and imports over a period of time. Two possibilities exist. First, when exports > imports, a country experiences a

Table 3.1 Level of trade for selected countries in 2020

Country	Level of trade (exports as % of GDP)
Argentina	18
Australia	22
Brazil	20
Canada	31
China	20
France	29
Germany	47
India	21
Japan	18
Mexico	41
New Zealand	23
South Africa	31
United Kingdom	28
United States	11

Source: World Bank, data.worldbank.org/indicator/NE.EXP. GNFS.ZS.

trade surplus. In this case, revenue generated from exports exceeds the cost of imports from the rest of the world. All else equal, when exports increase, domestic production rises. Producers increase their demand for economic resource inputs, including labor. Employment rises and unemployment falls. This increase in economic activity, however, may increase aggregate demand, the price level, and interest rates. Second, when exports < imports, a country experiences a **trade deficit**. Economists argue, however, that a trade deficit is not necessarily bad for an economy. When a country imports from the rest of the world, it is purchasing output from foreign producers. But a greater level of imports increases product variety and puts downward pressure on prices. Because trade flows include financial payments, they create flows of international **financial capital**, economic resources measured in terms of the money that businesses and entrepreneurs use for purchases.

Implications of a trade deficit

A trade deficit may contribute to a healthy and growing economy. Importing goods and services diversifies a country's consumption possibilities, creating a greater variety of choices for consumers. In addition, importing financial capital benefits a country if it uses the funds for productive investment opportunities, such as South Korea in the 1970s. If a country continues to borrow money from global capital markets, however, a trade deficit may weaken a country's economic position. First, if a borrower does not invest the funds productively, the country may struggle to make repayments. Second, foreign countries may seek higher interest rates, reducing the flow of financial capital in banking, real estate, and stock markets. Third, a trade deficit may lead to deindustrialization, the offshoring of jobs, a decrease in manufacturing employment, the closure of factories, and economic decline in industrial regions. An example of the latter is the United States during this century (Khanna, 2023).

Trade deficit: The case of the United States

Since 2000, the United States has experienced an annual trade deficit (Figure 3.1). Each year, the United States imports more goods and services from the rest of the world than it exports. While the country experiences an annual trade deficit, its GDP continues to grow. The problem, however, is that the United States continues to lose manufacturing jobs, as labor-intensive industries move to China, Mexico, and other countries (Autor et al., 2016).

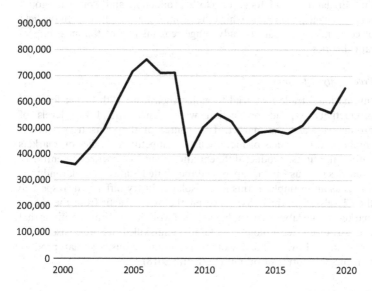

Figure 3.1 United States annual trade deficit (imports – exports) in millions of US dollars.

Source: Author using data from the Federal Reserve Bank of St. Louis, Fred.stlouisfed.org.

Sources of the gains from trade

International trade, the voluntary exchange of goods, services, and economic resources, creates economic gains. Trade increases both consumption and production possibilities. Sources of the gains from trade include the topics of the next four sections.

Comparative advantage

A country has **comparative advantage** in the production of some form of output if it can produce it at a lower domestic opportunity cost than its trading partners. A country has **absolute advantage** when it can provide more goods or services than other countries. Absolute advantage occurs with more economic resources and/or better technology. Trade between countries, however, should occur on the basis of comparative advantage. If a country specializes in the production of output in which it has comparative advantage, it minimizes its domestic opportunity cost. It then obtains other goods and services through trade. David Ricardo, the famous classical economist, writing in the early nineteenth century, argued that England and Portugal could both benefit by trading according to the principle of comparative advantage. Ricardo argued that England should focus on cloth production and Portugal should focus on wine production, which the countries eventually did. In the field of economics, comparative advantage remains one of the most important theories.

Productivity differences

International trade may lead to gains when firms with higher levels of productivity expand production while firms with lower levels of productivity exit the market. This source of the gains from trade – emphasized in models of monopolistic competition – relies on markets with many firms, product differentiation, and low barriers to entry. In countries such as China, Japan, and the United States, the solar industry serves as an example. Firms in the solar industry differ with respect to their levels of productivity; however, the firms benefit from the export market. In the labor market, high-skilled workers sort into positions that use advanced technology, while medium-skilled laborers use static technology. Lower-skilled workers sort into industries that produce non-fungible forms of output (Feenstra, 2018).

Price reduction

For many countries, international trade serves as a source of competitive advantage. Robert Feenstra (2018) analyzes the trade of sugar cookies between Denmark and the United States. In the absence of product variety or productivity differences between the countries, the only source of the gains from trade would be a price reduction accompanying the market entry of firms. This outcome would lead to a higher level of competition. The idea is that, in a market with a homogenous product and easy entry, economic profit in the industry equals zero before and after trade. As a result, a reduction in consumer price leads to a social gain. Unprofitable firms exit the industry. For this theory to hold, however, transportation costs must equal their true social value. If they do not, the economic resources devoted to transportation may lead to a social loss. With respect to this possibility, Joseph Shapiro (2016) calculates that the gains from trade are 100 times greater than the environmental costs of shipping.

Product variety

International trade is also beneficial when it increases the amount and variety of products. Examples include spices from southeast Asia, sugar from the Caribbean, and tea from India. Because these products result from optimal climate and soil, they reflect the ability of the exporting countries to rely on specialization and comparative advantage. But countries may trade varieties of products, even if they do not have fundamental differences. Examples of the latter include wine from France, cheese from the Netherlands, and automobiles from Japan. In these cases, economies produce differentiated varieties, meaning that the industries operate under conditions of monopolistic competition, not perfect competition (Feenstra, 2018).

Distributional consequences

Trade alters the supply of and demand for goods and services in the economy. As a result, producers may manufacture output for export markets. Consumers may purchase more imported goods and services. In addition, prices change, according to market conditions. These outcomes impact households with respect to their willingness and ability to purchase output. Households may be willing and able to consume a wider variety of goods and services. But trade may also lead to the outsourcing and offshoring of jobs. The implication is that trade alters consumption, production, and labor market conditions.

Consumption effects

Changes in consumption patterns reflect how economic welfare changes across households. All else equal, when the level of trade increases and households are able to consume more output, economic welfare rises. In export industries, an increase in exports leads to higher levels of employment. But when trade restrictions reduce household consumption, economic welfare declines. These restrictions may reduce employment in export industries.

Labor market effects

A labor market consists of the demand for labor by firms and the supply of labor by individuals. The interaction between supply and demand determines the equilibrium wage rate. In high-income countries, including the United Kingdom and the United States, the share of imports from the developing world rises over time. The reason is the ability of developing countries to employ low-wage workers. This process leads to an increase in the demand for labor in developing countries. As a result, labor markets in high-income countries that are "exposed to rising low-income-country imports ... experience increased unemployment, decreased labor-force participation, and increased use of disability and other transfer benefits, as well as lower wages" (Autor et al., 2013).

Effects on poverty

Trade alters the economic prospects of those living in poverty. Poverty stems from a lack of education, employment, and government support. From society's perspective, moving individuals out of poverty means improving both economic and social conditions. In developing countries, higher levels of trade create economic opportunities and conditions for poverty reduction. But a higher volume of trade increases the competition for manufacturing jobs. Developing countries compete for jobs in export-oriented manufacturing sectors. If a region that relies on manufacturing experiences the outsourcing or offshoring of jobs, the poverty rate rises.

Arguments against free trade

Even though economists normally argue for free trade, counter-arguments exist. The arguments against free trade focus on costs.

Countering foreign subsidies and dumping

One argument against free trade is that countries should counter the subsidies that foreign countries implement. In this context, a subsidy is a payment by government intended to assist a business in making the price of a good or service lower and more competitive. When foreign governments subsidize their businesses, the argument here is that the home country should do the same, in order to maintain a competitive global market. Another aspect of the argument focuses on the reality of dumping, when producers sell their output in foreign markets at lower prices, below production costs. This practice occurs when businesses experience recessionary intervals, face high domestic competition, or want to reduce inventories. In these situations, the businesses dump their output in foreign markets.

Infant industries

The infant industry argument states that countries should protect businesses in new and growing industries. A country may decide that if a particular industry has time to develop, it may reduce its production costs, increase efficiency, and eventually compete in the global market. Over time, businesses in the industry may employ technological advances. Aggregate supply may increase. With this policy, import restrictions occur, so the industry has time to grow. When the industry develops, the restrictions are eliminated. Domestic firms then compete in global markets. Examples of infant industry protection include automobiles, solar panels, and steel. The potential problem is that countries may maintain protections for too long. In this latter case, countries shield domestic producers from global competition, but do not provide the incentive for efficiency gains.

Protecting domestic jobs

In the global economy, firms settle in markets that provide the best opportunity for production, whether in developing or developing countries. Firms consider many factors, including infrastructure, level of education and training of the labor force, competition, collaboration, remote work, and resource costs. But global markets may create disadvantages for domestic producers. In industries such as clothing and electronics, firms outsource work to countries with lower production costs. Countries may respond by implementing policies that protect domestic jobs. The problem with these policies, however, is that firms experience the same competitive pressures. An economic race to the bottom may occur: firms move production to the areas with the lowest production costs.

Key terms

Absolute advantage
Balance of trade
Closed economies
Comparative advantage
Financial capital

Global production networks
Level of trade
Open economies
Trade deficit
Trade surplus

Questions

1 What are the economic implications of a trade surplus?
2 What are the economic implications of a trade deficit?
3 What are the sources of the gains from trade?
4 What are the distributional consequences of international trade?
5 What are the arguments against free trade?

References

Autor, D., Dorn, D. and Hanson, G. 2013. "The China Syndrome: Local Labor Market Effects of Import Competition in the United States." *American Economic Review*, 103(6): 2121–2168.
Autor, D., Dorn, D. and Hanson, G. 2016. "The China Shock: Learning from Labor-Market Adjustment to Large Changes in Trade." *Annual Review of Economics*, 8: 205–240.
Feenstra, Robert. 2018. "Alternative Sources of the Gains from International Trade: Variety, Creative Destruction, and Markups." *Journal of Economic Perspectives*, 32(2): 25–46.
Khanna, R. 2023. "America Should Once Again Become a Manufacturing Superpower." *Foreign Affairs*, 102(1), January/February. https://www.foreignaffairs.com/issues/2023/102/1
Shapiro, Joseph. 2016. "Trade Costs, CO_2, and the Environment." *American Economic Journal: Economic Policy*, 8(4): 220–254.
Vidya, C. and Prabheesh, K. 2020. "Implications of Covid-19 Pandemic on the Global Trade Networks." *Emerging Markets Finance and Trade*, 56(10): 2408–2421.
Vo, Thuy and Tran, Manh. 2021. "The Impact of Covid-19 Pandemic on the Global Trade." *International Journal of Social Science and Economics Invention*, 7(1): 1–7.

4 Trade policy

ESSENTIAL SUMMARY

The trade policy of a country consists of the laws, practices, and regulations that impact its exports and imports. Trade between the United States and China has been growing for decades, reflecting the high level of economic integration between the two countries. At the world equilibrium price, foreign quantity supplied – foreign quantity demanded = home quantity demanded – home quantity supplied. Trade policies such as tariffs, subsidies, import quotas, and voluntary export restraints alter trade patterns. Economists normally conclude that trade restrictions cause more economic costs than benefits. Around the world, production in the semiconductor industry benefits from targeted policy that encourages trade.

Trade between China and the United States

The trade policy of a country consists of the laws, practices, and regulations that impact its exports and imports. Trade policy includes the country's stance on international trade, whether it believes the domestic economy should integrate with the rest of the world through the global network of trade. China and the United States have an important relationship with respect to trade. Trade between the countries has been growing for decades, reflecting a high level of economic integration. The United States, for example, imports more output from China than any other country. For the United States, the benefits of this practice are lower consumer prices, higher household purchasing power, and access to China's market. But the costs are the loss of domestic manufacturing jobs due to import competition, national security concerns, and labor and human rights violations (Siripurapu and Berman, 2022).

DOI: 10.4324/9781003434900-5

The high level of trade between the countries did not always exist. For 30 years after the establishment of the People's Republic of China, in 1949, no trade between the countries occurred. After the normalization of relations between the countries, in 1979, trade grew from a few billion dollars' worth of output to hundreds of billions of dollars (Siripurapu and Berman, 2022).

According to the foreign trade account balances of the US Census Bureau, in nominal terms, the United States in the year 2000 exported $16.185 billion worth of output to China and imported $100.018 billion worth of output from China for an annual trade deficit of $83.833 billion. In the year 2020, the United States exported $124.543 billion worth of output to China and imported $432.683 billion worth of output from China for an annual trade deficit of $308.139 billion. As Figure 4.1 demonstrates, the US trade deficit with China has increased over time, although the deficit decreased in 2020. The trade balance demonstrates the high level of interconnection between the two countries.

Despite economic integration, a trade conflict has existed at times between China and the United States, resulting from three factors: the US trade deficit with China, competing economic systems, and trade barriers. The Chinese Communist Party oversees the country's economy in several ways, such as control of financial institutions, implementation of the country's economic planning commission, and

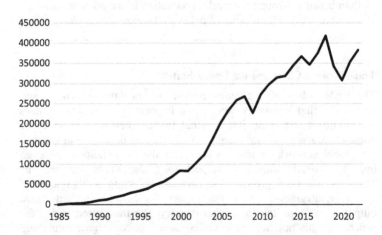

Figure 4.1 United States trade deficit with China (millions of nominal US dollars).

Source: Author using data from the US Census Bureau, https://www.census.gov/foreign-trade/balance/c5700.html.

management of state-owned businesses. China is more open to exports than imports from the United States.

In contrast, the decentralized nature of the US economy means that businesses are free to produce what they want, subject to budget constraints and market conditions. Individuals are free to consume their consumption bundles. Even though both economic systems attempt to increase living standards, the free market nature of the US economy leads to greater preferences for product variety and consumer choice. This reality contributes to the US trade deficit with China. In 2018–2019, the U.S. implemented taxes on Chinese imports, but China retaliated, raising the prices of US exports. The result of the trade war was twofold: US consumers experienced higher prices and aggregate real income decreased in both countries (Fajgelbaum and Khandelwal, 2022).

Model of import demand and export supply

Suppose a home country and a foreign country produce and trade a good without shipping costs. Assume the exchange rate between currencies is not a function of trade policy. Prices (P) are quoted in terms of the home currency. Trade results from price differentials between the two countries. If the price of a good in the foreign country is greater than the price in the home country, the home country will export the good, increasing the price at home until the price differential is eliminated. The world price and quantity traded depends on the export supply curve (XS) and import demand curve (MD).

In the foreign country, XS equals the difference between what foreign producers supply and what foreign consumers demand (Figure 4.2). At a price of P^1, foreign quantity demanded = foreign quantity supplied, so the quantity available for export equals zero. At P^2, foreign quantity supplied increases, but foreign quantity demanded decreases. At P^2, the horizontal

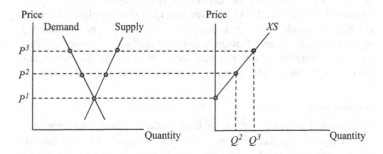

Figure 4.2 Export supply curve.

Source: Author.

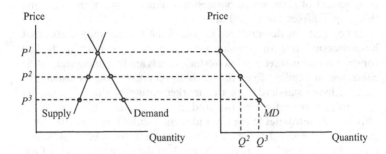

Figure 4.3 Import demand curve.

Source: Author.

distance between quantity supplied and quantity demanded represents the quantity of exports supplied (Q_2). At P^3, the horizontal distance between quantity supplied and quantity demanded increases, demonstrating that, at this price, the quantity of exports supplied rises to Q_3. Overall, the higher is the price, the greater is the quantity of exports supplied.

In the home country, MD is the difference between home consumer demand and home producer supply (Figure 4.3). At P^1, home quantity demanded equals home quantity supplied, and no imports occur. But at P^2, quantity demanded rises, reflecting the fact that consumers would rather buy more at a lower price; however, quantity supply falls, as producers sell less at a lower price. At P^2, import demand (Q_2) equals the horizontal distance between quantity demanded and quantity supplied. At P^3, the largest horizontal difference between quantity demanded and quantity supplied exists. At P^3, import demand equals Q_3.

The world equilibrium price (P^w) and world equilibrium quantity (Q^w) occurs where foreign export supplied equals home imports demanded (Figure 4.4). At P^w, foreign quantity supplied – foreign quantity demanded = home quantity demanded – home quantity supplied. Alternatively, foreign quantity supplied + home quantity supplied = foreign quantity demanded + home quantity demanded. That is, at P^w, world export supply = world import demand.

Consumer surplus

To evaluate the welfare effects of trade policies, economists determine the change in market efficiency. On the demand side, economists measure **consumer surplus** (*CS*), the difference between the market price for a good or service that consumers are willing and able to pay and what they actually pay. Consumer surplus measures the net benefit to

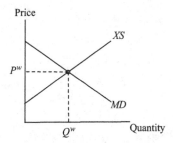

Figure 4.4 Equilibrium.
Source: Author.

consumers from market consumption. On a supply and demand graph, *CS* is the triangle above equilibrium price and below demand (Figure 4.5). When *CS* changes, the benefit to consumers from a trade policy increases or decreases.

Producer surplus

On the supply side, economists measure **producer surplus** (*PS*), the difference between the market price that sellers receive for the sale of a good or service and the price they are willing to charge. Producer surplus measures the benefit to sellers from market transactions. On a supply and demand graph, it is the triangle below equilibrium price and above supply (Figure 4.6). When *PS* changes, the benefit to sellers from a trade policy increases or decreases.

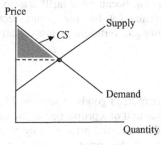

Figure 4.5 Consumer surplus.
Source: Author.

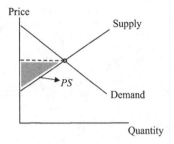

Figure 4.6 Producer surplus.

Source: Author.

Trade policies

Countries often rely on free trade, that is, the free flow of exports and imports based on market conditions. But they sometimes regulate trade flows with the following policies.

Tariff

A **tariff** (t) is a tax on imports, implemented to protect infant industries, decrease imports, and/or raise revenue. A tariff is either a fixed sum per unit or a proportion of the value of imports. When a country implements a tariff, the new price equals the world price plus the tariff ($P^w + t$). In the importing country, the world price is below equilibrium. At P^w, imports equal the horizontal difference between quantity demanded and quantity supplied. In Figure 4.7, the result of the tariff is to decrease the level of imports from Q^1Q^2 to Q^3Q^4. As a result, consumer surplus decreases by the area $a + b + c + d$ and producer surplus increases by the area a. Because the tariff is a tax on imports, it also generates tax revenue (c) for the public sector. Overall, the tariff creates a deadweight (efficiency) loss equal to area $b + d$.

Subsidy

An export **subsidy** (s) encourages the export of goods or services. Like a tariff, a subsidy is either a fixed sum per unit or a proportion of the value exported. While an export subsidy decreases the price paid by foreign importers, domestic consumers pay a higher price. The price in the exporting country increases from P^w to $P^w + s$ (Figure 4.8). In the exporting country, government has to pay the subsidy. With the subsidy,

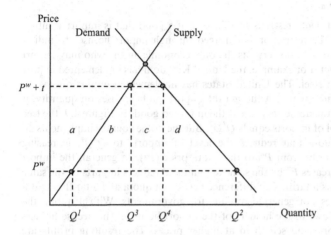

Figure 4.7 Effects of a tariff in the importing country.
Source: Author.

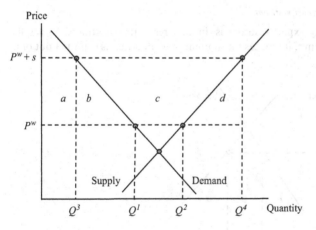

Figure 4.8 Effects of a subsidy in the exporting country.
Source: Author.

exports increase from Q^1Q^2 to Q^3Q^4. Consumer surplus decreases (a + b). The increase in price increases producer surplus (a + b + c). The subsidy costs government (b + c + d). Deadweight loss from the subsidy equals b + d.

Import quota

An **import quota** restricts the amount of a good that is imported into a country. The restriction is enforced through import licenses to individuals or firms, who serve as the only economic agents who may import the product. For example, the United Kingdom has implemented import quotas on steel. The United States has implemented import quotas on textiles and apparel. Although the import quota focuses on quantity, it increases the domestic price of the imported good. In Figure 4.9, the free trade level of imports equals Q^1Q^2. But the home country implements an import quota that reduces the level of imports to Q^3Q^4, increasing domestic price from P^w to the quota price (P^q). In general, the import quota increases P^w by the same amount and reduces imports by the same quantity as a tariff. The difference between a quota and a tariff is that a quota does not generate revenue for governments. With a quota, the revenue flows to the holders of the import licenses. The license holders buy imports and sell them at higher prices. The resulting profits are called quota rents. The loss to consumer surplus equals $a + b + c + d$. The gain in producer surplus equals a. Quota rents equal c. Deadweight loss equals $b + d$.

Voluntary export restraint

A **voluntary export restraint** is another restriction on trade. As a self-imposing limit, it reduces the amount of a good that is exported out of a

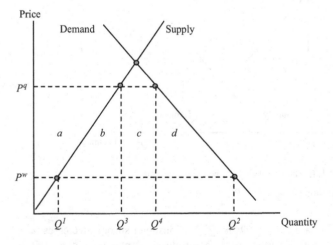

Figure 4.9 Effects of an import quota in the importing country.

Source: Author.

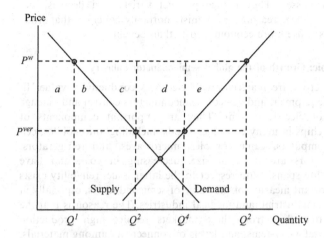

Figure 4.10 Effects of a voluntary export restraint in the exporting country.
Source: Author.

country. A famous example is the limitation by Japan of vehicle exports to the United States in the 1980s. In this case, the Japanese auto industry posed a threat to the US auto industry because of the popularity of fuel efficient and cheaper Japanese vehicles. Because of pressure from the government of the United States, Japan agreed to limit the export of these vehicles. In general, the exporting country chooses to implement the voluntary export restraint because it believes its trading partner could implement a more severe trade restriction as an alternative. In Figure 4.10, the exporting country reduces its level of exports from Q^1Q^2 to Q^3Q^4. Consumer surplus increases by $a + b$. Producer surplus decreases by $a + b + c + d + e$. Import licenses are assigned to the importing country, so quota rents (d) flow to the exporting country. Deadweight loss equals $c + e$.

The impacts of trade policy

Export subsidies alter market conditions, increasing domestic price, decreasing foreign price, and raising the quantity of exports. Trade restrictions such as tariffs, import quotas, and voluntary export restraints include different mechanisms to alter price or quantity. But the most important impact is the reduction in trade. These restrictions benefit one country or group at the expense of other countries or groups. In general, trade restrictions increase domestic prices for consumers, decrease quantities for producers, and create deadweight losses. They reduce product variety and decrease net income. For these reasons, economists normally conclude that trade restrictions cause more economic costs than benefits.

Special topic: Growth of the global semiconductor industry

Semiconductors are materials with electrical conductivity value. In electronic equipment and devices, semiconductors control and manage the flow of electric current. They are important components of electronic chips in many consumer goods, including automobiles, cell phones, computers, game consoles, microwaves, and refrigerators. Semiconductors are small in size, decreasing in cost, and have increasing life spans. With respect to the latter issue, reliability exists as an important measure of the value of semiconductors, especially in automotive, industrial, and medical industries. The reason is that the products that flow from these markets require high production standards, safety systems, and levels of connectivity among materials. Around the world, production in the industry benefits from targeted policy that encourages trade. Examples include trade agreements that strengthen supply chains, minimize the cost of economic resources, and encourage trade in both inputs and output.

Semiconductors were invented in the United States, but they have been around since the nineteenth century. In recent decades, the US government has used industrial policy in the form of demand supports, regulatory coordination, and supply incentives to encourage economic growth. Government purchasing and spending agreements reduce the risk of economic losses, encouraging investors to spend money on product development. For example, in 2023, the "Chips for America" program, with $50 billion in government outlays, provided financial motivation for semiconductor research, encouraged production in the industry, expanded manufacturing facilities, and highlighted concerns about the country's reliance on foreign chips (Swanson, 2023).

Industrial policies enable large businesses to scale up innovations and implement technological advances. The policies help small businesses experiment with new production processes. Laborers move through the industry, using the knowledge learned in one area to enhance production in other areas. Regulations for the transfer of technology ensure that innovations are shared between businesses of different sizes.

Even though the US semiconductor industry established itself as a global leader as recently as the 1990s, production and distribution occur on a global scale. Taiwan, South Korea, Japan, China, and the United States are the world's biggest producers. In this dynamic market, innovation occurs at all points on the global supply chain, benefitting from a diverse set of companies. In 2010, the global semiconductor industry produced almost $300 billion worth of output. In 2020, the industry produced more than $500 billion worth of output. With the demand for electronic chips increasing on a global scale, production will stem from growth in the automotive, data storage, and wireless industries (Burkacky *et al.*, 2022).

Key terms

Consumer surplus
Import quota
Producer surplus
Subsidy
Tariff
Voluntary export restraint

Questions

1 What characterizes trade between China and the United States?
2 In the model of import demand and export supply, what determines world equilibrium price and quantity?
3 How do trade policies work?
4 What are the overall impacts of trade restrictions?
5 How has trade policy helped the growth of the global semiconductor industry?

References

Burkacky, Ondrej, Dragon, Julia and Lehmann, Nikolaus. 2022. "The Semiconductor Decade: A Trillion-Dollar Industry." *McKinsey & Company*, April 1. https://www.mckinsey.com/industries/semiconductors/our-insights/the-semiconductor-decade-a-trillion-dollar-industry

Fajgelbaum, Pablo and Khandelwal, Amit. 2022. "The Economic Impacts of the US-China Trade War." *Annual Review of Economics*, 14: 205–228.

Krugman, Paul and Obstfeld, Maurice. 2014. *International Economics: Theory and Policy*, 10th Ed. New York: Pearson.

Siripurapu, Anshu and Berman, Noah. 2022. "The Contentious U.S.-China Trade Relationship." *Council on Foreign Relations*, December 2. https://www.cfr.org/backgrounder/contentious-us-china-trade-relationship

Swanson, Ana. 2023. "The CHIPS Act Is About More Than Chips: Here's What's in It." *The New York Times*, February 28. https://www.nytimes.com/2023/02/28/business/economy/chips-act-childcare.html#:~:text=Funding%20chip%20production%20and%20research,research%20into%20new%20chip%20technologies.

5   Trade agreements

ESSENTIAL SUMMARY

Trade agreements between countries establish trade guidelines and the flow of economic resources. With the objective of establishing economic integration, countries implement different types of trade agreements, including preferential trading areas, free trade areas, customs unions, common markets, economic unions, and monetary unions. The agreements, including the European Union (EU), U.S.-Mexico-Canada Agreement (USMCA), Mercosur, and the Association of Southeast Asian Nations (ASEAN), vary with respect to the role of trade flows, economic resources, currency, policy, and other characteristics.

The evolving nature of trade agreements

A **trade agreement** between countries establishes guidelines for trade in goods and services, barriers, and the movement of economic resources. These treaties define the rules of trade for all signatories. The main objectives of trade agreements are to increase the level of economic integration between countries and increase trade flows.

A country may establish multiple trade agreements with other countries, putting a domestic economy in a better position to compete in the global marketplace by reducing transportation costs and other impediments. Trade agreements simplify the process of exporting goods and services to trading partners. They establish a more transparent and predictable economic environment, boosting economic growth, the volume of trade, and the variety of goods and services available in the marketplace.

Although many regional trade agreements exist, the agreements that are discussed in this chapter include the European Union (1993),

DOI: 10.4324/9781003434900-6

U.S.-Mexico-Canada Agreement (2020), Mercosur (1991), and Association of Southeast Asian Nations (1967). These agreements go beyond trade flows to address multiple areas that impact trade, including investment, intellectual property rights, environmental quality, competition, and governance. The agreements establish an environment that enhances the economic relationship between countries. An interesting reality is that each of these trade agreements has experienced important changes, demonstrating their evolving nature.

With the EU, a major change occurred in 2020, when the United Kingdom withdrew, serving as the only country that has left the union. Since 1973, the UK was a member of the EU. But, in 2016, challenges including immigration, nationalist politics, and sovereignty led to a referendum in which a majority of individuals voted to leave the EU. The result led to volatility in financial markets, a political crisis, and economic turbulence as the process unfolded. Because membership in the EU provided economic benefits, withdrawal created competitive vulnerabilities for the UK.

In 2020, the U.S.-Mexico-Canada Agreement replaced the North American Free Trade Agreement (NAFTA). The new agreement established conditions for mutually beneficial trade between the three countries, creating conditions for economic growth in North America. The reason for the implementation of the new agreement was a campaign pledge by US President Donald J. Trump. Before he became president, Trump pledged to update NAFTA in ways that would put the United States in a more favorable economic position. From this perspective, the new agreement established stronger protections for worker rights, expanded markets for US farmers, and provided new rules for manufacturing. For businesses engaged in trade between the countries, the agreement increased stability in the market environment.

In 2016, the South American trading bloc Mercosur suspended Venezuela over human rights violations, finding that Venezuela had not included important economic and social regulations in its national laws. Joining the trading bloc in 2012, Venezuela experienced human rights abuses, soaring inflation, social instability, and hunger. Both economic and political conditions in the country motivated the founding members of Mercosur – Argentina, Brazil, Paraguay, and Uruguay – to suspend Venezuela. But this change did not hide the ongoing problems of the trade agreement, including the lack of a long-term strategy for economic growth and integration.

In 2021, the Association of Southeast Asian Nations announced the achievement of significant development goals, raising millions of people out of poverty among the member countries and improving access to healthcare and education. Drivers of change in the region, including demographics, economic activity, and migration, have improved economic conditions for member countries. The problem is that not everyone benefits from the process of integration. Low-income households have greater access to the global economy, but do not experience the benefits of stable employment and income generation.

Types of trade agreements

With the objective of establishing economic integration, countries implement different types of trade agreements. The agreements vary with respect to the role of trade barriers, flow of economic resources, currency, policy, and other characteristics.

Preferential trading area

A **preferential trading area** serves as the first stage of economic integration. It facilitates investment by easing regulations, reduces or eliminates trade barriers and restrictions on trade in goods and services, and exists between two or more countries. By establishing environmental goals, labor standards, and intellectual property rights, the agreement creates rules for international trade. The result is preferential access to markets for specific forms of output. But it also increases compliance costs, impacting the competitiveness of firms in foreign markets. An important characteristic of a preferential trading area is that it may be unilateral. That is, one country may reduce trade barriers without another country reciprocating. The reason is that access to the latter country's domestic market may exist as an important economic opportunity, despite the existence of trade barriers.

Free trade agreement

A **free trade agreement** exists as the second stage of economic integration, establishing a compact between member countries to implement few or no trade barriers and settle trade disputes. The difference between a free trade area and a preferential trade agreement is that the former does not contain a provision for unilateral trade. The characteristics of the free trade agreement apply to all member countries. For consumers, the free trade agreement increases product variety and decreases prices. For producers, the agreement establishes a larger market for sales. For countries, it encourages economic development by increasing living standards. The problem is that a free trade agreement may lead to job losses in certain industries as production moves to regions with comparative advantage. In addition, some companies suffer from a higher level of competition. As a result, while a free trade agreement creates conditions for economic growth, enhances efficiency, promotes innovation, and increases competitiveness, it impacts domestic industries in both positive and negative ways.

Customs union

A **customs union** serves as the third stage of economic integration. The idea is to enhance trade among member countries. Specifically, it decreases the administrative and economic burden of trade. It leads to the elimination of trade barriers such as customs duties, which are tariffs imposed on output that is transported across country borders. The objective is to decrease costs for both businesses and consumers. A customs union helps businesses allocate scarce resources, while attracting foreign direct investment into the economy. But, unlike free trade agreements, a customs union establishes a common tariff on imports from non-member countries. This policy makes trade among member countries more advantageous. In addition, countries in the union cannot establish their own trade agreements. The countries structure their economic arrangements in order to maximize the benefits of the customs union, but experience a lower degree of economic sovereignty. With this compact, member countries cannot protect infant industries through the implementation of trade barriers.

Common market

A **common market** exists as the fourth stage of economic integration. Known as a trading bloc, a common market eliminates internal trade barriers for member countries. It also implements common trade barriers for nonmembers. These characteristics are similar to a customs union. But the difference between a common market and a customs union is that a common market allows the free movement of economic resource inputs such as labor and capital between member countries. This flexibility encourages economies to allocate scarce resources to the most efficient uses. For example, domestic industries may require more labor than is available. By allowing labor to cross country borders, the common market contributes to the potential for economic growth. Industries compete for laborers across all member countries. For workers, the arrangement increases the size of the labor market, provides more economic opportunity, and enhances the likelihood of higher wages. For businesses, both economies of scale and productivity rise.

Economic union

An **economic union** exists as the fifth stage of economic integration, combining a customs union with a common market. An economic union eliminates trade barriers among member countries, creates common external trade barriers, and allows the free flow of economic resource inputs. The difference is that an economic union leads to the coordination of national economic policies. The integration of both fiscal and monetary policy means that member countries agree on government spending and methods of taxation. The benefit of an economic union is this integration, which allows member countries to experience a large market, policy coordination, and support. The cost, a lack of flexibility, means that member countries cannot deviate from the union's policy agreements, even if changing economic conditions require new methods. For example, one country in an economic union may experience recession but the others experience expansion. The struggling country would benefit from the implementation of expansionary fiscal and monetary policy, but the economic union may prohibit this policy at a particular moment in time.

Monetary union

The sixth and final stage of economic integration, **monetary union**, occurs when an economic union creates a single currency area with the introduction of common banknotes and coins. Historically, both economic and political considerations have led to a monetary union. From an economics perspective, a common currency eliminates the problem of exchange rate volatility, decreases transaction costs, enhances price transparency, and increases economic exchange. A common currency also creates a framework for a single monetary policy, implemented by a central bank for the union. Because representatives from each member country serve on policy boards, they have to work together to achieve the common goal of prosperity. The problem with monetary unions is that some countries may be vulnerable to external shocks because they cannot control their own monetary policies.

European Union

The EU exists as an economic and monetary union. With 27 member countries, the EU was created by the Maastricht Treaty of 1993, which established economic and political integration, common trade and security policy, and cooperation in domestic and foreign affairs. The agreement established oversight for the EU with respect to consumer protection, economic development, education, environmental protection, public health, and social issues. The Maastricht Treaty created a framework for the establishment of a common currency, the euro, which went into effect in 1999, and a monetary policy that applied to the union. The treaty established the rules that governed the conditions under which new members could join, including the level of public debt, rate of inflation, size of budget deficit, and stability of the exchange rate.

The treaty created new economic institutions, such as the European Central Bank, European Monetary Authority, and European System of Central Banks, which govern banking, economic, and financial activity.

But the precursor to the EU occurred in 1957 with six members (Belgium, France, Luxembourg, Italy, the Netherlands, and West Germany), who signed two Treaties of Rome, designed to establish a common market. In the 1950s, the idea of closer economic and political ties stemmed from the goal of integrating European countries after World War II. In the 1990s, 12 countries united to create an economic union, including the six original members plus Denmark, Great Britain, Greece, Ireland, Portugal, and Spain. In the twenty-first century, the EU expanded into central and eastern Europe. Great Britain, a founding member, exited the union in 2020 (Brexit), leading to the current number of countries. Today, the EU addresses challenges in the business environment, climate adaptation, democracy, energy, exchange rate stability, international trade, labor, regional conflicts, rule of law, and technological advances. Noteworthy are the proactive EU responses to the financial crisis of 2007–2008 and the coronavirus pandemic of 2020–2022.

The global financial crisis of 2007–2008, which began as banking and housing crises in the United States, created a major global downturn. Through a process of financial contagion, these problems led to a multidimensional crisis in the EU, including rising government debt, especially in Greece, a banking crisis, and macroeconomic instability. Some Eurozone countries struggled to service existing debts and finance budget deficits. As a result, the European Central Bank intervened, providing bailout loans. But the receiving countries had to agree to austerity measures, such as reducing government spending. The problem was that the austerity measures created conditions for social unrest, which persisted for years across the EU and reduced public trust in government institutions. The countries that financed the bailout programs – France and Germany – experienced majorities that opposed the program. The overall result was an extended period of economic uncertainty. But, in the end, the economic institutions of the EU managed to hold the union together and create conditions for economic recovery (Tosun et al., 2014).

The coronavirus pandemic of 2020–2022 complicated the economic environment. As Covid-19 spread, government institutions implemented a series of policies, including quarantines, household lockdowns, and economic shutdowns. Recovery from the crisis was slow, because variants of the novel coronavirus continued to appear. The EU implemented several strategies to fight the problem, including border controls, limitations on mobility, crisis coordination between countries, and the purchase of medical supplies and personal protective equipment. The EU institutions provided financial support to protect businesses and worker salaries, facilitating a return to normalcy. The crisis highlighted the need for cooperative methods to address external shocks that impact economies, households, and healthcare systems (Goniewicz et al., 2020).

U.S.-Mexico-Canada Agreement

On July 1, 2020, the USMCA went into effect as a free trade agreement, replacing the North American Free Trade Agreement. The USMCA governs trade flows in North America – worth more than $1 trillion annually – while preserving most of the NAFTA provisions that govern economic interaction between the three countries, such as competition policy, corruption, customs procedures, industry standards, and regulatory practices. Economists conclude that the 26-year existence of NAFTA led to larger trade flows and the integration of many industries between the three countries. But critics of NAFTA argue that the agreement led to losses in manufacturing jobs in the United States, particularly in the automotive industry.

In response, the USMCA, which helps to maintain the status of North America as one of the world's most productive and competitive regions, encourages the modernization of labor laws in Mexico, increases automobile production in the United States, and expands markets in Canada for Mexican manufacturing. In the United States, the USMCA protects intellectual property rights, strengthens agricultural trade among member countries, improves conditions for domestic workers, maintains the competitiveness of supply chains, and encourages innovation. In Canada and Mexico, the USMCA strengthens the mechanism for trade disputes and preserves their access to the economy of the United States. For all three countries, the USMCA maintains an economic environment with few barriers; however, compliance with the agreement creates administrative costs. The agreement establishes environmental and labor standards. Violations are subject to the trade dispute mechanism. The USMCA creates an economic framework in which Canada and Mexico continue to serve as top trading partners for the United States.

Overall, the USMCA perpetuates the growth in trade between the three countries, although the coronavirus pandemic in the early 2020s disrupted regional supply chains. The provisions to settle trade disputes are more advanced than those that existed under NAFTA. The framework addresses problems in the automotive, dairy, and solar industries. Over time, economists expect that the USMCA will continue to support one of the world's most vibrant trading regions.

Mercosur

The common market Mercosur includes permanent members and founders Argentina, Brazil, Paraguay, and Uruguay. In 1991, it began with the goals of improving relations between the countries, increasing trade and the movement of economic resource inputs, enhancing economic integration, and encouraging both economic development and democracy. The agreement eliminated customs duties, created a common external tariff on specific imports that come from outside the common market, and established a common trade policy for non-member countries.

As the chapter's introduction explains, Venezuela joined the common market in 2012, but the country was suspended in 2016 for a failure to maintain the agreement's democratic principles. Associate members of Mercosur include Bolivia, Chile, Colombia, Ecuador, Guyana, Peru, and Suriname, which experience lower tariffs when trading occurs with full members. These countries do not experience full access to all Mercosur markets or voting rights.

For Mercosur, 1991 to 1999 were the "golden years," because of the growing integration, trade flows, and economic gains (Campos, 2016). One reason was the decrease in trade barriers. Another reason was growing economic interdependence. A final reason was the growth of regional markets. For member countries, output per capita rose.

While Mercosur experienced these economic gains, problems emerged, starting in 2000. China's influence in the region grew. Fragmentation between member countries existed. Uneven trade with the rest of the world occurred. While the common market safeguarded industries, it also protected member countries from global competition, reducing their level of competitiveness. Additional challenges included business and political corruption, the establishment of trade agreements with other countries, internal divisions, policy mismanagement, unstable economies, and the difficulty of creating regional value chains. Diversification existed as a method to hedge against domestic and regional instability. Economic crises in the early 2000s and 2020s destabilized financial institutions.

In the current period, the common market's decision-making apparatus – consisting of groups that oversee economic and foreign arrangements – coordinates macroeconomic and trade policies and infrastructure projects such as bridges and highways. This coordination strengthens the ability of the member countries to experience positive economic outcomes. In addition, social integration increases cultural exchange and tourism. Political integration promotes democracy. Over time, the ability of Mercosur to exist as a beneficial trade agreement depends on whether the member countries continue to pursue policies of economic integration. Success also depends on the extent to which Argentina and Brazil provide leadership (Campos, 2016).

Association of Southeast Asian Nations

In 1967, the foreign ministers of Indonesia, Malaysia, the Philippines, Singapore, and Thailand signed an agreement to establish the ASEAN for the geopolitical reasons of security and peace; however, in 1992, the countries established the ASEAN trading bloc, which eliminated tariffs among member countries, increased economic integration, and served as a free trade agreement. Within a few years, Cambodia, Laos, Myanmar, and Vietnam joined, creating a regional market with more than 500 million people.

These countries vary with respect to their levels of economic development, resource endowments, technological capabilities, and trade volumes. Indonesia serves as a leader with its large population and level of economic activity, although Singapore and Malaysia experience a high volume of exports. Over time, attracting foreign direct investment (FDI) – especially from the EU, Japan, and the United States – has become an important objective (Chia, 2011). This type of investment establishes access to management expertise, markets, and technology, expanding opportunities for businesses and supply chains. The FDI also enhances economic integration between less developed and more developed countries through production networks and the allocation of labor to growing industries, especially electronics and automobile manufacturing.

The ASEAN prioritizes an economic environment that facilitates the flow of business investment, skills, and technology, aiming to establish transparent rules, regulations, and administrative processes. It also increases the region's production base, level of competition, and integration into the global economy. For the member countries, specific challenges include capacity building, economic engagement, institutional development, leadership, policy coordination, and resource mobilization (Chia, 2011). For countries in the ASEAN to continue to grow, they must focus on an increase in the flow of economic resources, high-quality institutions, human capital, labor productivity, management capability, and research and development.

Key terms

Common market
Customs union
Economic union
Free trade agreement
Monetary union
Preferential trading area
Trade agreement

Questions

1 Why do trade agreements evolve over time? What are some examples?
2 What are the types of regional trade agreements? How do they differ?
3 From a monetary perspective, what is unique about the European Union? Explain.
4 How does the U.S.-Mexico-Canada Agreement promote trade?
5 What are the benefits and costs of Mercosur?

References

Campos, Gabriela. 2016. "From Success to Failure: Under What Conditions Did Mercosur Integrate?" *Journal of Economic Integration*, 31(4): 855–897.

Chia, Siow. 2011. "Association of Southeast Asian Nations Economic Integration: Developments and Challenges." *Asian Economic Policy Review*, 6: 43–63.

Goniewicz, Krzysztof, Khorram-Manesh, Amir, Hertelendy, Attila, Goniewicz, Mariusz, Naylor, Katarzyna and Burkle, Frederick. 2020. "Current Response and Management Decisions of the European Union to the COVID-19 Outbreak: A Review." *Sustainability*, 12(9): 3838.

Tosun, Jale, Wetzel, Anne and Zapryanova, Galina. 2014. "The EU in Crisis: Advancing the Debate." *Journal of European Integration*, 36(3): 195–211.

6　International factor movements

ESSENTIAL SUMMARY

Labor mobility in a trade agreement such as a customs, economic, or monetary union provides a mechanism of adjustment for changing economic conditions. Labor mobility occurs less frequently than capital mobility, but labor mobility is an important characteristic of international economics. Global capital movements involve financial transactions, not the physical transfer of machines or equipment from one country to another. A foreign direct investment by an economic agent in one country means an investment that leads to controlling ownership in a business, asset, or form of real estate in another country.

Labor mobility

An important part of international economics is the study of the exchange of goods and services. But other forms of exchange occur. International factor movements involve the exchange of economic resources, such as labor migration and the transfer of capital through borrowing and lending. The principles of international factor movements are fundamentally the same as exchange of goods and services. As an example, consider labor mobility.

In a trade agreement, labor mobility provides a mechanism of adjustment for changing economic conditions. If a region experiences strong economic growth and a labor market shortage, workers move to the region, reducing the labor-market imbalance. In general, the flow of labor from one region to another or one country to another is driven by fluctuations in labor market conditions, impacting employment and wages. In the European Union, millions of people live and work in countries other than their countries of origin, while others envision

DOI: 10.4324/9781003434900-7

working abroad. The reasons for relocation include higher wages, culture, and economic opportunity. After laborers go abroad and work in a different country, they return with new experiences and skills. In the European Union, Bulgaria, Italy, Poland, Portugal, and Romania serve as important countries of origin. Germany, Spain, and Switzerland serve as common work destinations.

An important implication of the United Kingdom exiting the European Union in 2020 was the emergence of a labor market shortage, an example of how the country's departure reshaped the economy. While the coronavirus pandemic and rising energy prices disrupted the economy of the United Kingdom, Brexit impacted every sector. Following the withdrawal from the European Union, restaurants in London were short of staff, leading to fewer hours of operation and more hectic working conditions. The reason was that restaurants in London were used to recruiting bartenders, chefs, and servers from Greece, Italy, and Spain, but Brexit ended labor mobility to the United Kingdom from the European Union. For restaurants that stayed in business, many positions remained unfilled. The outcomes were fewer days of operation, the elimination of overtime, rising labor costs, and future uncertainty. There were even cultural ramifications: many young workers from Mediterranean countries viewed restaurant work in London as a rite of passage. The United Kingdom's post-Brexit policy of attracting higher-skilled laborers from Asia and Africa – not those who work in the restaurant sector – contributed to the labor shortage. To address the problem, the UK had to issue short-term visas to individuals from the continent (Landler, 2022).

International labor movements

At the country level, restrictions may exist on labor mobility. A country may prevent workers from seeking employment outside of its borders. But certain trade agreements, such as customs, economic, and monetary unions, allow labor mobility. As a result, while labor mobility occurs less frequently than capital mobility, it exists as an important characteristic of international economics.

Production of output

Suppose two countries, Home and Foreign, which produce a single form of output with two economic resource inputs: labor (L) and land (A). Assume labor mobility exists between the two countries. But land is fixed. In each country, output (Q) is function of economic resources: $Q = f(L, A)$. Because L and A are the only scarce resources, the level of output depends on the quantity of these inputs. The **production function**,

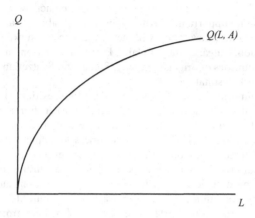

Figure 6.1 Production function.

Source: Author.

$Q(L, A)$, demonstrates the technological relationship between economic resources and the quantity of output, showing that output rises when the variable input – labor – increases, holding land constant (Figure 6.1).

Labor input

The slope of the production function reveals that, when more labor is added to production, output increases at a decreasing rate. This concept demonstrates the **marginal product of labor** (MPL), which is the change in output that results from a one-unit change in labor input. As Figure 6.2 reveals, when more labor is employed, MPL decreases. That is, as the ratio of labor to land rises, the MPL falls. As a country employs more labor, it uses more labor-intensive forms of production.

For each unit of labor, the real wage equals labor's marginal product. This condition holds true for perfectly competitive markets. The area under MPL equals total output. The total payment to labor equals the level of employment (L^1) times the real wage. The remainder equals land rents, income earned by land owners for which there is a fixed supply.

The impact of labor mobility

Assume the two countries have identical production technology, but differ with respect to their labor-land ratios. Because labor is more abundant in Home, workers in Foreign earn higher real wages, while land at Home earns higher rents. With this difference, an incentive exists

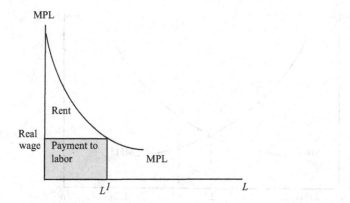

Figure 6.2 Diminishing marginal product of labor.

Source: Author.

for workers in Home to move to Foreign. Land owners in Foreign would like to move their land to Home, but land is fixed.

Suppose the two countries establish a trade agreement that allows labor movement: some workers move from Home to Foreign. The result is that, at Home, the labor force decreases and the real wage increases. In Foreign, the opposite occurs. Without restrictions on labor mobility, this process continues until the MPL is equal in the two countries.

Figure 6.3 shows this process, demonstrating the causes and effects of labor mobility. The horizontal axis includes the total labor force of both countries. On the left-hand side, the vertical axis measures the MPL for workers in Home. On the right-hand side, the vertical axis measures the MPL for workers in Foreign. For both countries, employment increases with a movement toward the middle of the graph.

At Home, the initial level of employment equals $0^H L^1$. In Foreign, the initial level of employment equals $0^F L^1$. The result of this initial allocation of labor is that the real wage is lower in Home (point C) than Foreign (point B). Because workers may move freely between the countries, some laborers move from Home to Foreign and receive higher real wages. The process continues until real wages converge across countries (point A). The distance $L^1 L^2$ equals the level of labor migration from Home to Foreign.

In addition to wage convergence, two other results occur. First, world output increases. Home's output decreases by the area under MPL^H from L^1 to L^2. Foreign's output increases by the area under MPL^F from L^1 to L^2. Because the latter is larger, world output rises. The total gain in

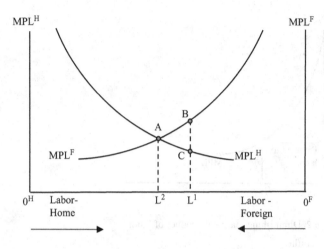

Figure 6.3 Labor mobility.

Source: Author.

output is equal to the triangle ABC. Second, even though world output rises, not everyone shares in the gains. While workers who move from Home to Foreign receive higher real wages, those who stay in Home receive lower real wages. Moreover, the landowners in Foreign benefit from an increase in the labor supply. Landowners in Home do not. Overall, international labor mobility may potentially benefit all workers; however, in practice, some groups benefit at the expense of others.

Labor mobility and trade

The economic model demonstrates that international labor movements are a function of differences in economic resources and relative wages. Like international trade, labor movements lead to an increase in world output, but the benefits are not equally distributed. If the countries produce two forms of output, and one is more labor-intensive, international trade exists as an alternative to factor mobility. While Home exports the labor-intensive good, it may import the land-intensive good. In this scenario, an equalization of factor prices could eliminate the need for international labor mobility. However, in the global economic environment, while trade may serve as a substitute for labor mobility, it is not a perfect substitute. A number of reasons exist. Countries may not allow their laborers to work in other countries. Trade barriers may exist. Economic resources may differ across countries.

Technological capabilities may vary. The implication is that trade in economic resources occurs for the same reason as trade in output: to secure an economic gain (Krugman and Obstfeld, 2009).

International capital movements

Capital movements involve financial transactions, not the physical transfer of machines or equipment from one country to another. These transactions exist as an important feature of international economics. They include many types of transactions, such as banks in the United States lending to Canadian firms, residents in Japan buying stocks in South Korea, or firms in the United Kingdom investing through their subsidiaries in other countries. With the first example, international borrowing and lending exists as international exchange. It serves as **intertemporal trade** in which lending and borrowing creates an opportunity for future spending. In the following model, suppose two countries, Home and Foreign, produce one form of output.

Home's production

Home's production possibilities curve (PPC) demonstrates a bias toward present consumption (Figure 6.4). Home produces a level of output equal to Q. But it consumes at a level equal to D. How is this possible? Given the shape of the PPC, the price of future consumption is higher in Home than in Foreign. Therefore, Home imports future consumption. That is, Home borrows to finance future consumption. The idea of

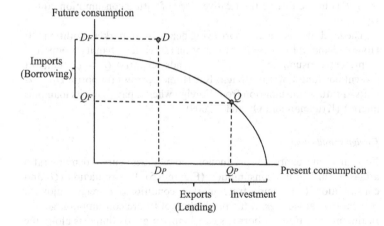

Figure 6.4 Home's economic position.

Source: Author.

intertemporal trade is that economies do not consume all of their output in the present. Some of the output exists as investment in the form of buildings, computers, equipment, and machines. By allocating some economic resources today for this productive capital, economies are able to produce more in the future. But as economies divert more economic resources from present consumption to future consumption, the production of present consumption (Q_P) decreases and the production of future consumption (Q_F) increases. A tradeoff therefore exists. The more an economy invests today in productive capital, the more it will be able to produce in the future. [In Figure 6.4, as Q_P moves leftward on the horizontal axis, Q_F moves upward on the vertical axis.] But lower levels of current investment lead to lower levels of future economic growth. The tradeoff exists between current and future consumption.

What is the price of future consumption? A country may trade in terms of borrowing and lending. When a country borrows, it consumes at a level greater than production. Over time, however, when it pays back the principal of the loan plus interest, it consumes at a level less than production. Therefore, the country's tradeoff for a higher level of current consumption is less future consumption.

Assuming no changes in the price level, the price of future consumption refers to the real interest rate (r), which is the price of borrowing. When borrowing occurs, the country has the ability to undertake more present consumption with the condition that it must repay its loan. That is, the future repayment is $(1 + r)$ times the level of borrowing. As r increases, the quantity of borrowing decreases, and vice versa. Because the country's tradeoff equals a unit of current consumption for the price of $(1 + r)$ in the future, the relative price of future consumption equals $1/(1 + r)$.

The level of lending and borrowing depends on market conditions. If Home's demand for present consumption (D_P) is less than its production of present consumption (Q_P), Home lends (exports) $Q_P - D_P$ units of present consumption to Foreign. But Home borrows (imports) $D_F - Q_F$ units of future consumption from Foreign when it pays back its loan plus interest (Krugman and Obstfeld, 2009).

Foreign's production

Foreign's intertemporal production possibilities curve demonstrates a bias toward future consumption (Figure 6.5). Its production (Q) and consumption (D) demonstrate market conditions. Foreign enjoys a comparative advantage in the production of future consumption goods. In the present, Foreign borrows consumption goods (imports along the horizontal axis), repaying the loan with consumption goods produced in the future (Krugman and Obstfeld, 2009).

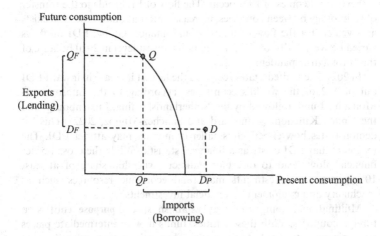

Figure 6.5 Foreign's economic position.

Source: Author.

Overall, equilibrium in the global market demonstrates two conditions. First, Home's level of exports of present consumption (lending) equal Foreign's level of imports (borrowing). Second, Home's level of imports of future consumption (borrowing) equal Foreign's level of exports (lending). To establish these equilibrium positions, the interest rate adjusts.

Foreign direct investment

A **foreign direct investment** (FDI) by an economic agent in one country means an investment that leads to controlling ownership in a business, asset, or form of real estate in another country. In economies around the world, FDI impacts a country's level of economic growth. The reason is that FDI leads to the accumulation of physical capital and transfer of human capital to receiving countries.

The link between FDI and economic growth is important in a world of internalization of production processes and deindustrialization of developed countries. In this process, technology transfer enhances the productivity of economic resources, which lowers the technology gap between international and national firms and between developing and developed countries. But when countries have lower levels of human capital and struggle to absorb new technology, FDI has a less significant role in production. Depending on whether FDI flows evenly across sectors in economies, FDI may increase inequality (Alvarado et al., 2017).

Several outcomes of FDI occur. The flow of FDI leads to the transfer of technology between countries, increases international trade, and exists as a vehicle for the flow of international finance. Global FDI outflows varied between 2010 to 2020, falling to its lowest level in 2020 because of the coronavirus pandemic.

In 2021, the United States recorded the largest increase in inward FDI out of 112 of the world's economies, according to the International Monetary Fund, followed by the Netherlands, China, Luxembourg, and the United Kingdom (Damgaard and Sanchez-Munoz, 2022). This list demonstrates how effectively smaller economies may attract FDI. The reason is that FDI exists as a financial statistic. While the cross-border financial flows lead to direct or indirect ownership share of at least 10 percent, the investments may fund economic resources such as machinery and equipment or financial investments.

Multinational companies may establish **special-purpose entities** in foreign countries. With these entities, funds flow to intermediate places on their way to final destinations. The entities take advantage of regulatory or tax benefits in the overseeing countries, inflating FDI statistics. But the entities do not have direct links to real economies.

When FDI links directly to real economies, it serves as an engine of economic development. FDI impacts economies by creating access to global markets and production networks, linkages between firms, knowledge spillovers, higher managerial skills, new production processes, and training for employees. For countries, the effect of these factors is to diversify exports, alter employment, raise production, and transform the pattern of production. As a result, for economies of all sizes, an incentive exists to attract FDI (Alfaro, 2016).

Scarcity

In many countries, a scarcity of financial capital for new investment exists as a reason for the attraction of FDI. Foreign investors assess the global economic environment and make FDI decisions, leading to the establishment of economic opportunities in local markets. The economic agents may not want to take control over foreign companies, but choose instead to invest in markets. In this context, countries with more developed financial markets attract more FDI. Foreign investors may hedge against exchange-rate volatility by borrowing from foreign banks. But this process may crowd out local firms by limiting their ability to borrow (Alfaro, 2016).

Economic linkages

Economic linkages between firms and markets impact FDI. The more developed a local financial market is, the greater is the ability of entrepreneurs to start firms or expand their production processes. As business creation and expansion flows to other sectors, financial markets facilitate linkages between foreign and domestic firms, transforming into FDI spillovers. In particular, FDI correlates with higher growth rates in countries that have more advanced financial markets. At the micro level, these economic opportunities enhance business productivity. Over time, the reallocation of resources may contribute to the decline of specific industries. In the presence of economic gains, countries may treat foreign firms with financial incentives and tax breaks. The impacts of FDI are therefore conditional on domestic economic conditions (Alfaro, 2016).

Conditions for growth

The impact of FDI is greater when country resources are invested in education, infrastructure, worker training, financial markets, and the reduction of technology gaps. When FDI occurs alongside local investment, firms benefit. The idea is that FDI diversifies exports, provides resources to markets, and strengthens industrial capacity. But the relationship between FDI and production may occur in both directions. When FDI enhances production, economic growth attracts future FDI (Alvarado et al., 2017).

Key terms

Foreign direct investment
Intertemporal trade
Marginal product of labor
Production function
Special-purpose entities

Questions

1 In the United Kingdom, why did Brexit create a labor market shortage?
2 Why is international labor mobility similar to international trade?
3 What are international capital movements?
4 Why is foreign direct investment an important aspect of economic integration?
5 How does foreign direct investment impact economies?

References

Alfaro, Laura. 2016. "Gains from Foreign Direct Investment: Macro and Micro Approaches." *The World Bank Economic Review*, 30(S1): 2–15. 10.1093/wber/lhw007

Alvarado, Rafael, Iniguez, Maria and Ponce, Pablo. 2017. "Foreign Direct Investment and Economic Growth in Latin America." *Economic Analysis and Policy*, 56: 176–187.

Damgaard, Jannick and Sanchez-Munoz, Carlos. 2022. "United States Is World's Top Destination for Foreign Direct Investment." *IMF Blog*, December 7.

Krugman, Paul and Obstfeld, Maurice. 2009. *International Economics: Theory and Policy*. Boston: Pearson Addison Wesley.

Landler, Mark. 2022. "Where's My Waiter? U.K. Restaurants Scramble for Staff After Brexit." *The New York Times*, December 22.

7   International monetary system

ESSENTIAL SUMMARY

During the coronavirus pandemic, the World Bank, an international financial institution, supported vaccine rollouts in more than 100 countries. Before World War I, the gold standard provided global financial stability. But instability in the interwar period with currency devaluations, protectionism, and unstable exchange rates led to calls for change. The Bretton Woods system, created after World War II, established an adjustable exchange rate framework with the US dollar as the world's main currency. While the Bretton Woods system combined the advantages of a gold standard with fixed exchange rates, its downfall reflected an overvaluation of the US dollar. Bretton Woods was replaced by the floating exchange rate system that exists today. A special topic in the chapter is the growth of digital currency, important for the study of global monetary economics.

World Bank support during the coronavirus pandemic

During the coronavirus pandemic, the World Bank, an international institution that provides grants and loans to low- and middle-income countries, supported regions around the world. The pandemic was disrupting the global economy, supply chains, and health systems. A particularly important area of need was the distribution of vaccines. In 2021, more than a year after the initial spread of the novel coronavirus, many low-income countries struggled to obtain and disseminate vaccines. Pre-existing problems included weak infrastructures, limited capacity, and inefficient logistical systems. But daily infections and deaths were rising. The World Bank stepped in to help. The institution supported vaccine rollouts in more than 100 countries, worth billions of

DOI: 10.4324/9781003434900-8

US dollars. The financing from the World Bank funded the procurement and distribution of vaccines, training of health workers, expansion of storage capacity, engagement of citizens, and strengthening of health systems. The institution provided aid to individuals in high-need areas, helping to slow the spread of the novel coronavirus and its variants.

International monetary system

The global monetary system is characterized by **floating exchange rates**: currency values are determined by the forces of supply and demand in the foreign exchange market. In this system, government controls and trade restrictions do not restrain floating exchange rates. Changes in currency values are determined in the marketplace. The value of the British pound relative to the US dollar, for example, fluctuates freely in the market. As a result, a tourist from the United Kingdom wishing to travel to the United States must check the pound value of the dollar to forecast how much the trip will cost. If the value of the pound increases relative to the dollar, the trip will be less expensive. If the value of the pound decreases relative to the dollar, the trip will be more expensive. Overall, a floating exchange rate system adjusts to global economic conditions, when currency values fluctuate in the marketplace. If a country's economy is stable, its currency is normally stable. But if a country's economy is unstable, its home currency may decrease in value, reflecting economic conditions. In the latter situation, the central bank may have to intervene in the foreign exchange market to stabilize the value of the home currency.

The case for floating exchange rates

The argument for the floating exchange rate system reflects the preference for flexibility. As economic conditions change, the market alters currency values. This flexibility puts a floating exchange rate in position to serve as an automatic stabilizer, helping to promote the internal and external balances of countries. Internal economic balance refers to economic growth and full employment. External balance refers to a stable exchange rate and trade flows. With floating exchange rates, central banks do not have to intervene in the marketplace, unless the currency experiences wide fluctuations. With floating exchange rates, the world does not require a main currency such as the US dollar to facilitate global monetary conditions.

The case against floating exchange rates

The argument against the floating exchange rate system focuses on the potential for instability. Rapidly changing currency values may lead to large fluctuations in the international monetary position of countries. If a home currency rapidly decreases in value, economic agents may struggle to purchase imports. In this context, central banks may implement inflationary policies, freed from the obligation of fixing the value of the domestic currency relative to other currencies. In addition, currency speculation may lead to destabilizing outcomes if economic agents sell a country's currency. One outcome of this action is unpredictable changes in international prices. Another outcome is the illusion of central bank autonomy. If currency values fluctuate in an unpredictable manner, central banks may feel the need to intervene in the foreign exchange market. Finally, uncoordinated economic policies resulting from floating exchange rates sometimes lead to beggar-thy-neighbor outcomes. This occurs when the policies of a home country that address internal balance worsen the economic problems of other countries.

Gold standard and interwar years

The **gold standard** period (1870–1914) was characterized by the ability of countries to maintain both internal and external balance. Having its origin in the nineteenth-century ability of individuals to use gold as a medium of exchange, unit of account, and store of value, central banks preserved the official rate of exchange between gold and currency. To maintain currency values, central banks had to hold a sufficient level of gold reserves. In this environment, internal balance meant stable prices and full employment. External balance meant stable currency values. Because currency values were tied to gold, a surplus or deficit in a country's **balance of payments** – the sum of the current account balance, capital account balance, and nonreserve component of a country's financial accounts – had to be financed by the shipment of gold between central banks. But historical evidence reveals that the gold standard did not automatically lead to stability.

A country's balance of payments provides a record of its international transactions with the rest of the world. The balance of payments includes both payments to foreign agents (debits) and receipts from foreign agents (credits). In the balance of payments, three types of international transactions exist. First, the exports and imports of goods and services are recorded in a country's current account. Second, transactions from purchases and sales of financial assets are recorded in the financial account. Third, the transfer of wealth between countries in nonfinancial, nonproduced, or intangible assets is recorded in the capital account as inflows and outflows. With the balance of payments, every entry is recorded twice, once as a debit and once as a credit.

During the interwar years (1918–1939), different balance of payments positions emerged. During World War I, governments suspended the gold standard. Many countries financed their war efforts by printing money. Productive capacity and labor forces decreased because of losses during the war. Inflationary pressures persisted. After World War I, many countries returned to the gold standard, including the United States in 1919 and the United Kingdom in 1925. When the Great Depression began, in 1929, countries had to scramble to address the problem of rising unemployment. In 1931, the United Kingdom left the gold standard. In 1933, the United States left the gold standard, before returning to it in 1934. During this time, countries that refused to devalue their currencies but maintained the gold standard experienced economic problems. One reason for the global nature of the depression was the gold standard itself. By turning within, many countries in the 1930s chose to focus on their internal balance, reducing trade with the rest of the world. By decreasing the gains from trade, however, they created high costs for the global economy, prolonging the depression. As of 1939, many economies were still struggling. During that year, World War II began in Europe.

New international monetary order

The devastation of World War II created the incentive for a new international monetary order. The **Bretton Woods** system was named after the town in New Hampshire where a global monetary conference was held in 1944. The system served as a compromise between the British plan of John Maynard Keynes, the world's pre-eminent economist, for an international central bank and the American plan of Harry Dexter White, a senior US Treasury Department official, for a global stabilization fund. The compromise established an adjustable peg system with the US dollar serving as the world's reserve currency.

The system attempted to avoid the problems of the interwar period: currency devaluations, protectionism, and unstable exchange rates. Between the world wars, federal governments struggled to maintain both fixed exchange rates and free trade. But they wanted internal stability. The Bretton Woods system provided a framework in which countries could establish full employment and economic growth while maintaining external balance in trade.

Convertibility

At the Bretton Woods conference, representatives from 44 countries agreed that the US dollar would be convertible into gold at $35 per ounce. Every other currency in the system was then fixed in value to the dollar. In addition, the currencies of member countries were convertible into each other. In this context, a **convertible currency** is one that may be bought or sold in the foreign exchange market with few transaction costs or restrictions. This meant that a British citizen who purchased US dollars could sell them in the foreign exchange market for pounds, buy US exports, travel to the United States, or sell them to the Bank of England, the central bank.

The convertibility of the US dollar in the Bretton Woods system established the dollar as the world's main currency. The dollar was held in large quantities by central banks around the world. The fact that the dollar was convertible into other currencies meant that much of the world's international trade was denominated in dollars. The dollar emerged as an international medium of exchange, unit of account, and store of value.

The overall goal of the Bretton Woods system was to combine the advantages of a gold standard with fixed exchange rates, establishing stability in the international monetary system. Member countries held international reserves in dollars or gold, having the right to exchange dollars with the United States Federal Reserve for gold at the official price. Because the US Treasury guaranteed the dollar-gold link, foreign holders of dollars were reassured that their reserves were stable. But two inconsistencies emerged during the Bretton Woods era.

Inconsistencies

The first inconsistency stemmed from the gold standard. When the growth in global output exceeded global gold production, the relative price of gold needed to increase. But the Bretton Woods system maintained fixed exchange rates. This reality led to a period of deflation with the price of gold fixed at $35 per ounce. With negotiation, countries in the system besides the United States could devalue their currencies to maintain internal price levels, but the United States could not. In the 1960s, two developments held off the deflationary problem: an increase in Russian gold sales and the development of South African gold mines. In 1968, the problem was resolved with the implementation of a two-tier gold market, which allowed the non-official price of gold to fluctuate. The result was that the US dollar and currencies pegged to the dollar became fiat currencies, not backed by gold or any other physical commodity (Obstfeld, 2013).

The second inconsistency remained after the creation of the two-tier gold system. The official tier maintained the US obligation to exchange foreign dollar reserves for gold at the official rate. But growth in both the global production of output and dollar reserves outpaced global gold production. It became clear that if the US Treasury were to keep the

$35 buying price for gold, the US stock of gold would decrease. Eventually, the United States failed to hold a sufficient amount of gold to redeem the official foreign dollar reserves. The United States was vulnerable to a run by central banks. It became clear that the fixed exchange rate system did not offer enough flexibility. The value of the dollar needed to fluctuate in the open market. The reason was that, in the Bretton Woods framework, it was overvalued (Obstfeld, 2013).

Fall of Bretton Woods

On August 15, 1971, the demise of the Bretton Woods system began. On this date, US President Richard M. Nixon suspended the dollar's convertibility into gold. At the end of 1971, the Group of Ten industrialized countries announced a new system of exchange rates with a devalued dollar. The problem with this decision was that dollar devaluation existed as a difficult process for the United States. Because the dollar served as a numeraire currency, the US could devalue the dollar only if all other countries increased the value of their currencies against the dollar. These actions required multilateral negotiations, which many countries did not advocate because appreciation in the value of their currencies made their exports more expensive.

In early 1973, another economic outcome weakened the system: speculative pressure devalued the dollar further in the fixed exchange rate system, without efforts of central banks around the world to maintain the Bretton Woods requirements. When the Group of Ten established a system in which six European Union countries would tie the value of their currencies together, allowing them to jointly fluctuate against the dollar, the Bretton Woods system ended. Overall, the problem was that the Bretton Woods system of fixed exchange rates did not allow countries to achieve both external and internal balance. Adjustable exchange rates were necessary. In 1973, the movement to an adjustable exchange rate system was viewed as temporary. But the movement ushered in the floating exchange rate system that has persisted to this day.

The current system

The current international monetary system, which has evolved since the 1970s, is characterized by the central role of the US dollar in global economics, fluctuating exchange rates, growing capital flows, and openness to trade. This system has provided flexibility in response to crises and global shocks. It has contributed to the growth of the networks of globalization, higher levels of international trade, and global economic interdependence.

Looking ahead

The appearance of the financial crisis of 2007–2008 and the coronavirus pandemic of 2020–2022 means that global financial risks remain. Therefore, it is important to continue to strengthen the global monetary system. At the country level, current account imbalances exist, emphasizing the need for floating exchange rates. Because the US dollar (and to a lesser extent the pound, euro, and yen) continues to exist as an important global currency, economic activity in the United States has spillover effects in other countries, impacting economic choices, financial markets, and currency valuations. In addition, volatility in capital markets and liquidity shocks (shortages of money) exist as contemporary features of the international monetary system. These problems establish the need for cooperation, crisis management, and effective governance.

Special topic: The growth of digital currency

A special topic in the global monetary system is digital currency. Modern economies thrive because economic agents specialize in the production of certain goods and services, trading with others who specialize in the production of different goods and services. Money facilitates this exchange. When a particular form of money is divisible, durable, and scarce in a predictable way, it facilitates exchange. Money such as fiat currency, which has value because the government issuing it declares it to be legal tender, serves as a unit of account, store of value, and medium of exchange. In growing economies with efficient monetary systems, a fiat currency promotes prosperity and stability. But another important function of money is the ability to facilitate transactions. Digital currency, such as **cryptocurrency**, undertakes this function in an efficient and instantaneous manner. Digital currency merges traditional features of money with the efficiency of digital transactions.

Certain digital currency networks, including Bitcoin, are decentralized. These networks have developed as alternative forms of money. A growing acceptance of digital currency has made it possible to undertake transactions that are not linked to traditional sources of value or bank accounts. These forms of money are not a part of formal monetary systems. They exist in unregulated markets. Once touted as alternatives to traditional currencies and central banking, cryptocurrencies experience systematic risk. Even though these systems create networks of economic agents, the monetary values may experience wide fluctuations, eliminating their ability to hedge against price-level changes.

Computers running cryptocurrency networks serve as nodes, maintaining the updated log of digital currency ownership. The decentralized record of ownership in a peer-to-peer network exists as a **blockchain**, facilitating the exchange of digital currency from one agent to another.

With Bitcoin, an individual agent who sells digital currency to someone else must provide a key that demonstrates consent to the transaction. The software encrypts each transaction, but a public record is kept across the network.

An important part of the system is that buyers and sellers remain anonymous, but transactions exist in the public realm. As a result, exchange requires a private key among the buyer and seller and a public key in the network. After transactions occur, the network updates ownership, providing the mechanism for the system to operate (Wheelan, 2016).

Other digital currencies exist, including Amazon Coins, Facebook Credits, and Microsoft Points. These currencies are not a claim on real assets but are issued by businesses that want to facilitate economic activity in computing, social networking, video gaming, and other areas. While these examples exist as methods to increase transactional efficiency, linking the buyer to the seller, they evolve with the functioning of the platform. The digital currencies exhibit network effects when their value increases when more agents use them (Gans and Halaburda, 2013). The digital currencies are independent of state-issued currency; however, they are useful in providing a greater understanding of monetary systems. Exchange occurs between agents when they accept digital currencies and participate in their platforms.

Key terms

Balance of payments
Blockchain
Bretton Woods
Convertible currency
Cryptocurrency
Floating exchange rates
Gold standard

Questions

1 During the coronavirus pandemic, why did the World Bank provide aid to countries?
2 What characterizes the current global monetary system?
3 Before Bretton Woods, what were the characteristics of the international monetary system?
4 What were the characteristics of the Bretton Woods system? What led to its demise?
5 Why has digital currency grown in importance?

References

Gans, Joshua and Halaburda, Hanna. 2013. "Some Economics of Private Digital Currency." In Goldfarb, Avi, Greenstein, Shane and Tucker, Catherine (Eds.), *Economic Analysis of the Digital Economy*. Chicago: University of Chicago Press.

Obstfeld, Maurice. 2013. "The International Monetary System: Living with Asymmetry." In Feenstra, Robert and Taylor, Alan (Eds.), *Globalization in an Age of Crisis: Multilateral Economic Cooperation in the Twenty-First Century*. Chicago: University of Chicago Press. 301–342.

Wheelan, Charles. 2016. *Naked Money: A Revealing Look at Our Financial System*. New York: W. W. Norton & Company.

8 Foreign exchange market

ESSENTIAL SUMMARY

An exchange rate is the price of one currency in terms of another. During the coronavirus pandemic, a rise in confirmed cases increased exchange rate volatility for countries, but government interventions offset this trend. Exchange rates are important for international trade because they determine the prices of output denominated in foreign currencies. With the supply of and demand for currency, the foreign exchange market involves buying, selling, and exchanging currencies. Equilibrium is the exchange rate that equates the quantity of currency demanded with the quantity of currency supplied. The market is in equilibrium when deposits in all currencies possess the same rates of return. A factor that impacts the exchange rate is the relative prices between two countries: exchange rates reflect relative purchasing power, which is captured in the concept of purchasing power parity. The balance of trade, productivity, and expectations also impact currency values.

The pandemic and exchange rate volatility

An **exchange rate** is the price of one currency in terms of another. When going to Spain, a tourist from Mexico must exchange Mexican pesos into European euros at the current level of exchange. Most currencies, including pesos and euros, fluctuate in the marketplace, rising or falling according to supply and demand conditions. The study of exchange rates is important because of their relationship to international trade. When a home country's currency decreases in value in a process of **depreciation**, the country's exports become less expensive. In contrast, an increase in value of a home country's currency in a process of **appreciation** makes

DOI: 10.4324/9781003434900-9

the country's exports more expensive. Over time, the relationship between currency values and trade flows helps to determine a country's balance of trade.

Because of its disrupting characteristics, the coronavirus pandemic reduced trade and altered economic conditions. The pandemic also impacted **exchange rate volatility**, the risk that is associated with unexpected movements in the exchange rate. When a country's exchange rate is stable with respect to other currencies, fluctuating within a predictable band, a country's foreign trade tends to be stable. But exchange rate volatility – when a currency increases or decreases in value in an unpredictable manner – may lead to unforeseen outcomes in other areas of the economy. A sudden and large depreciation in a home currency, for example, may lead to rising inflation and more expensive imports. Volatility may also intensify financial market risk, increase uncertainty with respect to foreign investment, and reduce social welfare.

The coronavirus pandemic existed as a shock to the global economy. The novel coronavirus spread in human transmission networks, increasing confirmed cases around the world, first in developed countries and then in developing countries. Government responses, including restrictions on population movements and transportation controls, led to disruptions in the global economy, such as a decrease in the volume of international capital flows. Research on the relationship between the coronavirus pandemic and exchange rate volatility concluded that a higher level of confirmed cases intensified exchange rate volatility, but the interventions implemented by governments to counter the effects of the coronavirus pandemic suppressed exchange rate volatility. At the country level, the interaction of these two effects determined the level of exchange rate instability (Feng et al., 2021).

Exchange rates and international trade

Exchange rates are important for international trade because they determine the prices of output denominated in foreign currencies. Economic agents in the United States import works of art, collectors' pieces, and antiques from the United Kingdom. On an annual basis, the aggregate value of this category of imports is in the hundreds of billions of British pounds.

Exports from the United Kingdom to the United States

Suppose an individual in the US wants to import a painting from the UK, which is priced at £1000. The individual wants to know how much the painting costs in US dollars. To make the calculation, the individual must multiply the price of the painting in pounds by the price of a pound in terms of dollars. The latter is the dollar's exchange rate with respect to the pound. If the exchange rate is $1.25 per pound, the dollar price of the painting is:

$(1.25 \text{ \$/£}) \times (£1000) = \$1,250.$

If the \$/£ exchange rate changes, the dollar price of the painting increases or decreases. For example, if the pound depreciates against the dollar, falling to 1.15 \$/£, the price of the painting would decrease in terms of dollars:

$(1.15 \text{ \$/£}) \times (£1000) = \$1,150.$

In contrast, if the pound appreciates against the dollar, rising to 1.35 \$/£, the price of the painting would increase in terms of dollars:

$(1.35 \text{ \$/£}) \times (£1000) = \$1,350.$

The implication is that a currency depreciation makes a home country's output less expensive for foreigners. But a currency appreciation makes a home country's output more expensive for foreigners. These are the reasons that exchange rates are important for a country's position with respect to international trade.

Exports from the United States to the United Kingdom

Changes in the exchange rate also alter prices that economic agents in the UK pay for US products. When the exchange rate is $1.25 per pound, the pound price of a $500 cellphone from the US is:

$(\$500)/(1.25\text{\$/£}) = £400.$

When the pound depreciates to $1.15 per pound, the dollar appreciates. In this situation, the cellphone from the US becomes more expensive for a buyer in the UK:

$(\$500)/(1.15 \text{ \$/£}) = £435.$

When the pound appreciates to $1.35 per pound, the dollar depreciates. The cellphone from the US becomes less expensive for a buyer in the UK:

$(\$500)/(1.35 \text{ \$/£}) = £370.$

In sum, when a home country's currency depreciates, its exports become less expensive, but imports become more expensive. In contrast, when a home country's currency appreciates, its exports become more expensive, but imports become less expensive. In the foreign exchange market, these serve as important principles.

Market for foreign exchange

The market mechanism brings together buyers and sellers for the purpose of exchange. The **foreign exchange market** determines exchange rates between currencies. The market includes buying, selling, and exchanging currencies. On the demand side of the market, several participants exist, including central banks, commercial banks, corporations, individuals, and nonbank financial institutions. These economic agents buy and sell foreign exchange, their transactions differing by economic value. For example, when individuals buy foreign exchange for tourism, the transaction exists as a small fraction of trading in the marketplace. In contrast, commercial banks exist in a pre-eminent position in the foreign exchange market, as most international transactions involve bank deposits denominated in foreign currencies.

In financial centers around the world, such as Frankfurt, London, New York City, Singapore, and Tokyo, trillions of dollars of foreign exchange are traded each day. Currency traders use sophisticated software programs to look for **arbitrage** opportunities. They buy a currency at a lower price and sell it for a higher price. If the pound were selling for $1.15 in London and $1.25 in New York City, a currency trader could purchase £1 million for $1.15 million in London and sell it for $1.25 million in New York City.

Because all traders would seek this opportunity, however, the market would soon adjust, as an increase in demand for pounds in London would increase the price in that location, and an increase in supply of pounds in New York City would decrease the price there. That is, the market would soon eliminate the opportunity for arbitrage. In reality, the integration of global financial centers makes arbitrage opportunities brief, lasting a few seconds before the market adjusts.

As the predominant currency facilitating global financial flows, the US dollar serves as a medium of exchange between currencies. On a global scale, most transactions between commercial banks involve US dollars, because the dollar exists as the world's **vehicle currency**, the currency most often used to invoice international currency transactions. A commercial bank, for example, may want to sell Chinese yuan and buy Japanese yen. An exchange rate exists between these currencies. But the commercial bank may sell the yuan for dollars and then use the dollars to buy yen. The use of US dollars involves an additional step, but the transaction cost for currency exchange is normally lower when the transaction is denominated in dollars.

Spot and forward transactions

Exchange rate transactions such as those in the previous examples occur "on the spot," when economic agents agree to exchange bank deposits in immediate deals. These spot transactions use spot exchange rates, current market prices that traders pay to purchase other currencies. But currency traders may wish to lock in an exchange rate for a future transaction. In this latter case, the traders use forward exchange rates, which specify the price of exchange rate transactions at a future date. Because a currency trader may lock in a future transaction date for 30 days, 90 days, 180 days, or another length of time, the trader may hedge against the potential for volatility in the exchange rate market. The benefit of this approach is that forward exchange rates hedge against the possibility that a home currency will depreciate in value over time, increasing the cost of a foreign currency in the future. Speculators also use currency futures. If they expect that a currency will appreciate over time, they purchase futures contracts and gain from the transaction.

The demand for foreign exchange

The demand for foreign exchange is similar to the demand for goods and services. An economic agent may purchase foreign currency for practical purposes when it is needed or speculative purposes when it may increase in value. An important factor in this consideration is expectations. An economic agent interested in purchasing foreign currency must consider two factors: the interest rate and the change in value against other currencies. With the first factor – the interest rate – deposits in banks pay interest because they are loans from depositors. A deposit means a corporation, financial institution, or individual is lending currency to a bank and not using it for another purpose. At a pound interest rate of 0.05 (5 percent per year), a purchase of £10,000 would yield £10,500 after one year. With the second factor – the expected change in the exchange rate – currency traders in a home country, for example, the United States, estimate how many dollars they will get back over time after an initial purchase of foreign currency. Suppose the pound appreciates (dollar depreciates) in value over the course of a year, going from $1.00 per pound at the beginning of the year when buying occurs to $1.20 per pound at the end of the year when selling occurs. If the individual buys the pound low and sells the pound high, the individual will have a positive return in dollars.

Rate of return from holding an asset

The rate of return of holding currency or any asset is the increase in value that occurs over time. Suppose an individual in the United States is evaluating whether or not to purchase pounds. The dollar rate of return from holding pounds equals the pound interest rate (i_p) plus the rate of appreciation of the pound relative to the dollar. The latter is calculated by taking the dollar/pound exchange rate expected to exist a year from today ($E^e_{\$/\pounds}$) and subtracting today's dollar/pound exchange rate ($E_{\$/\pounds}$). If the pound appreciates against the dollar, ($E^e_{\$/\pounds}$) − ($E_{\$/\pounds}$) > 0, contributing positively to the rate of return from holding pounds. If the pound depreciates against the dollar, ($E^e_{\$/\pounds}$) − ($E_{\$/\pounds}$) < 0, reducing the rate of return from holding pounds.

With respect to financial decisions, the individual in the United States must compare the rate of return from holding dollars to holding pounds (or other currencies). In the United States, the rate of return from holding dollars is equal to the dollar interest rate (i_d). As a result, if the expected dollar rate of return (i_d) > the expected pound rate of return [i_p + ($E^e_{\$/\pounds}$) − ($E_{\$/\pounds}$)], the individual should hold dollars. But if i_d < [i_p + ($E^e_{\$/\pounds}$) − ($E_{\$/\pounds}$)], the individual should hold pounds.

Suppose the interest rate in the United Kingdom and United States equals 4 percent in each country (Table 8.1). Suppose no transaction costs exist from exchanging dollars for pounds. For an individual in the United States holding dollars, i_d is the dollar rate of return. (column 2). But, for an individual in the United States, the pound rate of return equals the pound interest rate (column 3) plus the change in value of the pound against the dollar (column 4). In cases 1–3, the dollar rate of return (column 2) < the expected pound rate of return (column 5), so the individual should hold pounds. In cases 4–6, however, the dollar rate of return > the expected pound rate of return, so the individual should hold dollars. Whether the individual should hold dollars or pounds depends on the expected change in currency value.

Equilibrium in the foreign exchange market

The rate of return is important for determining whether economic agents will hold foreign currencies. It is also important for understanding the concept of equilibrium in the foreign exchange market, the point in

Table 8.1 Rate of return in dollars and pounds

(1) Case	(2) Dollar rate of return (i_d)	(3) Pound interest rate (i_p)	(4) Rate of pound appreciation (positive) or depreciation (negative)	(5) Expected pound rate of return [(3) + (4)]	(6) Hold dollars or pounds?
1	0.04	0.04	0.05	0.09	Pounds
2	0.04	0.04	0.03	0.07	Pounds
3	0.04	0.04	0.01	0.05	Pounds
4	0.04	0.04	−0.01	0.03	Dollars
5	0.04	0.04	−0.03	0.01	Dollars
6	0.04	0.04	−0.05	−0.01	Dollars

Source: Author.

which the foreign exchange market settles. In particular, equilibrium is the exchange rate that equates the quantity of currency demanded with the quantity of currency supplied. With respect to the rate of return, the foreign exchange market is in equilibrium when deposits in all currencies possess the same rates of return.

From the perspective of the United Kingdom, suppose the supply of dollars (determined by the flow of UK exports to the US and US central bank policy) and the demand for dollars (determined by economic agents in the UK wanting to purchase US goods and services or travel to the US) in Figure 8.1. The equilibrium exchange rate of £1= $1.25 may be written equivalently as $1 = £0.8. Moving up on the vertical axis means an appreciation of the dollar and depreciation of the pound (dollars have a higher price in pounds and pounds have a lower price in dollars).

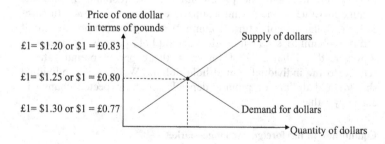

Figure 8.1 Supply of and demand for dollars in the United Kingdom.

Source: Author.

When an exchange rate fluctuates, it is known as a floating exchange rate or freely fluctuating exchange rate. On a global scale, this is the most common arrangement. In this situation, changes in supply and demand determine exchange rate fluctuations, when a currency appreciates or depreciates in value. Changing economic conditions shift the supply curve, demand curve, or both.

Shifts in demand

A change in demand for a foreign currency is a function of changing demand for the country's exports, its level of inflation, and interest rates. For example, if economic agents in the UK experience a greater desire to purchase US exports, the demand for dollars will increase. In addition, if US inflation decreases or US interest rates increase, the demand for dollars in the UK rises. As an example, suppose US interest rates increase. This raises the rate of return on dollar-denominated assets, so the demand for dollars in the UK increases from D^1 to D^2 in Figure 8.2. As a result, the dollar appreciates and the pound depreciates.

Shifts in supply

From the perspective of the United Kingdom, the supply of dollars is derived from both UK exports to the United States and policies of the US central bank. When UK exports increase, the inflow of dollars also increases. In addition, if the US central bank buys US bonds in the open market, the supply of dollars increases. In either case, the supply curve of dollars shifts to the right from S^1 to S^2 in Figure 8.3. As a result, the dollar depreciates and the pound appreciates.

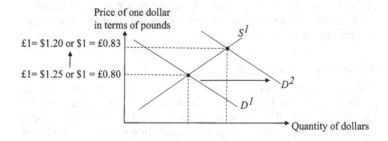

Figure 8.2 Increase in the demand for dollars.

Source: Author.

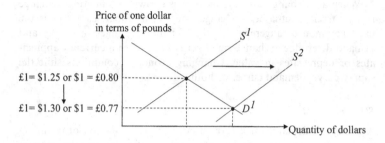

Figure 8.3 Increase in the supply of dollars.

Source: Author.

Purchasing power and relative prices

A powerful factor in impacting the exchange rate is the relative prices between two countries. The reason is that exchange rates reflect relative purchasing power, which is captured by **purchasing power parity** (PPP). The theory states that, if $1 buys the same amount of goods and services in the United States as £1.25 in the United Kingdom, then the long-run equilibrium exchange rate should be $1 = £1.25. In its simplest form, PPP asserts that the exchange rate between two currencies equals the ratio of the price levels between the two countries. The famous "Big Mac Index" of The Economist (2023) magazine, published since 1986, serves as an informal method to verify the PPP theory. For example, if a Big Mac costs £3.79 in the United Kingdom and $5.36 in the United States, the implied exchange rate is 3.79/5.36, or $1 = £0.71. But if the actual exchange rate is $1 = £0.81, the Big Mac Index demonstrates that the dollar is overvalued and the pound is undervalued. The exchange rate should adjust. An economy's price level entails a market basket of goods and services, so the Big Mac Index serves as an approximation of reality.

Balance of trade and productivity

Exchange rates reflect a country's balance of trade and level of productivity. If the United States experiences a trade deficit with the United Kingdom, the supply of dollars in the UK increases, causing the dollar to depreciate against the pound. In contrast, if the United States experiences a trade surplus with the United Kingdom, the supply of dollars in the UK decreases, causing the dollar to appreciate against the pound. In addition, an increase in productivity in a home country's tradable goods sector, relative to the other country, would cause the home country's currency to appreciate. Because the productivity of business investment would also increase, direct foreign investment would flow into the home country, further increasing the value of the currency.

Expectations

Expectations impact currency values. If economic agents expect the central bank of a home country to increase the money supply through expansionary policy, they may forecast inflationary pressure. These events characterize the United Kingdom, the United States, and other countries during the aftermath of the coronavirus pandemic. In this case, economic agents anticipate a depreciation in the value of the home currency, so they sell the home currency, and the value declines before inflation occurs. Other factors such as an expectation of rising production costs, salaries, or expansionary fiscal policy could lead to a similar result.

Key terms

Appreciation
Arbitrage
Depreciation
Exchange rate
Exchange rate volatility
Foreign exchange market
Purchasing power parity
Vehicle currency

Questions

1 If a home currency appreciates, what happens to its flow of exports and imports?
2 If a home currency depreciates, what happens to its flow of exports and imports?
3 In the foreign exchange market, what happens to the value of a home currency if the demand for the currency increases? Show this example on a graph.
4 In the foreign exchange market, what happens to the value of a home currency if the supply of the currency increases? Show this example on a graph.
5 With respect to exchange rates, explain the concept of purchasing power parity.

References

The Economist. 2023. "Our Big Mac Index Shows How Burger Prices Are Changing." *The Economist*, January 26. https://www.economist.com/big-mac-index

Feng, G., Yang, H., Gong, Q. and Chang, C. 2021. "What Is the Exchange Rate Volatility Response to COVID-19 and Government Interventions?" *Economic Analysis and Policy*, 69: 705–719.

9 Developing countries and the global economy

ESSENTIAL SUMMARY

Low-income countries struggle to establish an economic framework necessary for economic development, the process in which a country enhances the living standards of its people. Developing countries share common objectives, including the desire to increase the material well-being of their citizens. Economies include the formal sector and informal sector. While the former is monitored and taxed by governments, the latter is not. Developing countries are characterized by high levels of economic inequality, the unequal distribution of income and opportunity among individuals in a country. Global poverty entails the state of deprivation in which individuals do not have access to the resources and basic necessities they need to live healthy lives. The most important environmental problem facing the world is climate change, the long-term shifts in both temperatures and weather patterns

Manufacturing

According to the World Bank, developing countries have low-income and middle-income economies. A discussion of this income classification exists in chapter 1. Table 9.1 includes a partial list of countries. While the countries vary with respect to their levels of development, some common features exist. Low-income countries struggle to establish an economic framework necessary for **economic development**, the process in which a country enhances the living standards of its people. Some common reasons include ineffective governance, a lack of investment in education and training, and an inability to create the markets necessary for job creation. Middle-income countries have more advanced markets,

DOI: 10.4324/9781003434900-10

Table 9.1 Examples of developing countries

Low-income countries	Lower-middle-income countries	Upper-middle-income countries
Afghanistan	Bangladesh	Albania
Eritrea	Bolivia	Argentina
Ethiopia	Cameroon	Brazil
Guinea	Ghana	Bulgaria
Liberia	Haiti	China
Madagascar	Honduras	Colombia
Malawi	India	Costa Rica
Mali	Indonesia	Jamaica
Niger	Kenya	Jordan
Rwanda	Nepal	Malaysia
Sudan	Nicaragua	Mexico
Uganda	Sri Lanka	Peru

Source: World Bank, https://datatopics.worldbank.org/world-development-indicators/the-world-by-income-and-region.html.

economic infrastructures, and economic policies than their low-income counterparts, but they often struggle with conflict, fragility, and an inability to reduce poverty.

The process of development

In the process of economic development, does manufacturing serve as an important factor? The old view in the field of economics was that manufacturing and industrialization were synonymous with economic development. Countries began with large agrarian sectors. But growing economies increased the demand for economic resources. The process of manufacturing led to foreign direct investment, businesses and industries, and economic growth. In the eighteenth century, the United Kingdom served as the first industrializer, followed in the nineteenth century by Belgium, France, Switzerland, and the United States. During the twentieth century, Germany, Japan, and Russia industrialized their economies. Over time, industrialization continued around the world, establishing a model for economic development.

But the modern view in the field of economics is that, in successful economies, the service sector accounts for a sizable portion of gross domestic product, existing as an important element in the process of economic growth. But a close examination reveals that, for many countries, the elements of economic growth stemming from the service sector include specific industries, including business processing, finance, software, and tourism. China and South Korea serve as recent exceptions because of their large manufacturing bases. But India exists as an example of a country whose service sector growth links to its process of economic development.

Services

Regions of the world develop according to different areas of the economy: agriculture (A), industry (I) – construction, manufacturing, mining, and utilities – manufacturing (M), and services (S). Compared to developing economies, developed economies increase the size of their service sectors at a faster rate. In addition, in developed economies, the service sector constitutes a larger share of the national economy. In both categories, the historical data demonstrate that, as agriculture decreases as a share of the economy, the service sector increases.

Characteristics

Developing countries are diverse in culture, economies, history, politics, and social conditions. But developing countries with large economies may struggle with cohesion and efficiency while benefiting from large markets, economic resources, and access to global networks. Developing countries with small economies may struggle with limited economic resources and skills, experiencing fewer opportunities to access global networks of exchange. China, for example, with its large population and important place in the global economy, is much different than Bolivia, with its small economy and land-locked population. But developing countries share common objectives, including the desire to increase the material well-being of their citizens. They attempt to establish stronger economies through employment and production. They try to reduce poverty and inequality with greater access to resources and opportunity. They attempt to provide better access to education, health, and housing through social programs and services. In many developing countries, problems include climate change, a dependence on foreign resources and technology, environmental degradation, inadequate economic opportunities, income disparities, inefficient education and healthcare systems, international debt problems, poverty, and unemployment. The next four sections discuss some important common problems.

Climate

The most important global environmental problem, **climate change**, is the long-term shift in both temperature and weather patterns. The problem stems from human activity. The burning of fossil fuels – coal, natural gas, and oil – leads to carbon dioxide (CO_2) emissions, which persist in the atmosphere. These emissions rose for decades until the

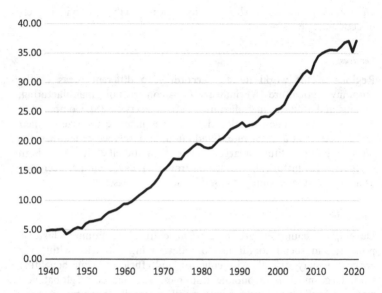

Figure 9.1 Annual global CO_2 emissions in gigatons.

Source: Author using data from Our World in Data, https://ourworldindata.org/co2-emissions.

onset of the coronavirus pandemic in 2020, a year in which the world emitted more than 35 gigatons of CO_2 (Figure 9.1). The problem is that a higher concentration of CO_2 and other greenhouse gases in the atmosphere distorts the planet's energy balance, strengthening the greenhouse effect, raising average global temperatures, and increasing the frequency of extreme weather events. Compared to previous human transformations of natural systems, such as agriculture and mining, climate change stands apart in its complexity, economic significance, and scale. While the process of fossil-fueled industrialization raises millions of people out of poverty, the climate externality poses significant problems, including inequitable outcomes and climate disruptions (Hsiang and Kopp, 2018).

Inequitable outcomes

Even though the poorest countries in the world contribute a small percentage of the CO_2 emissions to the world's total, they suffer disproportionately from a warming planet. Eighty percent of all greenhouse gases flow from 20 countries. More than 40 percent flows from China and the United States. The problem is that increasing frequencies of drought, floods, and heat stress are forecasted for the remainder of the century. The world's less developed countries already face challenges with respect to economic vitality, environmental quality, and social stability. The risks of climate change, including food and water insecurity, are unevenly distributed among the world's poorest people, leading to new inequities and the exacerbation of inequities that already exist. Without policies that manage and prepare for the changing climate, the health risks for vulnerable populations will increase. The largest problems will exist in regions with higher levels of exposure and susceptibility, including rising morbidity and mortality, heat waves, storms, infectious diseases, negative health impacts from drought and wildfires, and respiratory diseases from declining air quality (Ebi and Hess, 2020).

Climate disruptions

Climate disruptions alter economic activity, impacting the ability of developing countries to integrate into the global economy. Developing countries in Africa, for example, are projected to experience extensive climate change outcomes. The need for methods of adaptation from communities, regions, and national governments is apparent; however, methods of adaptation experience constraints. Countries may struggle to obtain the economic resources necessary to implement appropriate solutions. In developing countries, four main concerns about adaptation exist: climate models are insufficient to provide the knowledge necessary to strengthen food systems and household livelihoods; adaptation responses are often fragmented and limited with respect to connection with local expertise; adaptation strategies often ignore broader development challenges; and resources for adaptation are insufficient. Together, these challenges demonstrate the severity of the climate problem (Adenle et al., 2017).

Informality

Economies include the **formal sector** and **informal sector**. While the former is monitored and taxed by governments, the latter is not. Informal businesses undertake activities that have market value, so they would contribute tax revenue to governments if they were recorded. Examples of informal sector jobs include domestic workers, home-based workers, informal sales of domestic crops, street vendors, subsistence farmers, and waste pickers. According to the International Monetary Fund, around 60 percent of the world's employed population ages 15 and older, about two billion individuals, have worked in the informal sector (Delechat and Medina, 2020). The informal sector has several characteristics.

Size

Relative to the size of the economy, the informal sector is large. Employment in the informal sector often comes from self-employed individuals living near subsistence levels, which constitutes millions of people in developing countries. Many other forms of informal sector activity exist, including peddlers, small furniture businesses and repair shops, and transportation services. Most of these individuals do not comply with regulations or register with local governments. They undertake transactions in cash, avoiding the banking sector and tax system. Other economic agents, larger in scale, hide some of their sales from the public sector, reducing tax payments. These forms of economic activity are present in all countries, especially those that are developing (La Porta and Shleifer, 2014).

Productivity

Businesses in the informal sector are often small. While formal sector firms employ dozens or hundreds of workers, informal sector businesses normally employ one or a few workers. Often informal economic activity consists of a single person offering a good or service in the marketplace. In addition, informal sector businesses normally offer little **value added**, the difference between the market value of output and the sum value of its intermediate inputs. In the formal sector, a firm may add value to a product through marketing and advertising. In the informal sector, little of this activity exists. The implication is that wages for informal sector workers are significantly less than their formal sector counterparts, an indication of low productivity (La Porta and Shleifer, 2014).

Financing

Regulation does not oversee informal sector businesses. Individuals in the informal sector struggle from an inability to own land or office space, largely because the workers roam the streets for their work or occupy their premises illegally, fearing eviction. Other challenges include an inability to access markets and raw materials, bribes, and a lack of opportunities with formal sector firms and government agencies. An important problem in the informal sector is the inability to access financing. Because of a lack of connection with local governments and the banking system, informal sector businesses and individuals cannot obtain loans. In developing countries, banks will not lend to businesses or individuals that lack accounting and registration. In many developing countries, an exception is **microfinance**, the financial services by governments, non-profit institutions, or financial agencies provided to low-income groups, businesses, or individuals, who are excluded from the banking sector. Most microfinance transactions entail the establishment of credit in the form of microloans (La Porta and Shleifer, 2014).

Transition

Informal sector businesses rarely move into the formal sector. In countries around the world, most firms that begin in the formal sector start out as registered firms. Informal businesses exist in the informal sector without experiencing an opportunity to switch. Consistent with this outcome, informal sector businesses rarely sell their output to firms in the formal sector. They lack a connection. The outcome is that informal sector businesses occupy an economic space that rarely connects with the formal sector. In response, many countries have simplified the process of registration by establishing outreach efforts, lowering the cost of registration, providing information, and implementing enforcement visits. The results are mixed. Few informal sector businesses join the formal economy. They avoid regulation and taxes, but benefit when they receive microloans (La Porta and Shleifer, 2014).

Development

When countries develop, informal sector businesses become less important. For higher-income countries, the informal sector constitutes a smaller percentage of the economy, compared to their lower-income counterparts. As per capita income increases, the share of informal economic activity decreases. As countries develop, both educational and economic opportunities rise. When the formal sector grows, individuals operating in the informal sector have the opportunity to move to formal sector employment (La Porta and Shleifer, 2014).

Inequality

Developing countries are characterized by high levels of **economic inequality**, the unequal distribution of income and opportunity among individuals. In addition to the economy, inequality may extend to education, gender, health, and nutrition. The problem is that the individuals who suffer from inequality may also struggle to climb out of poverty, establish stable incomes, increase their living standards, and work in the formal sector. For a country, the outcome is the inability to extend the process of economic development to all members of society. While methods to reduce inequality include changes in economic and social norms, closing gaps in education and health, inclusive patterns of economic growth, redistributive policies, and effective leadership, developing countries often struggle to establish a more equal distribution of income and opportunity.

Table 9.2 Countries with the highest Gini coefficients

Country	Gini coefficient	Status
South Africa	63.0	Upper-middle income
Namibia	59.1	Upper-middle income
Suriname	57.9	Upper-middle income
Zambia	57.1	Low-income
Sao Tome and Principe	56.3	Lower-middle income
Central African Republic	56.2	Low-income
Eswatini	54.6	Lower-middle income
Mozambique	54.0	Low-income
Brazil	53.4	Upper-middle income
Belize	53.3	Upper-middle income

Sources: World Bank, https://worldpopulationreview.com/country-rankings/gini-coefficient-by-country, https://datahelpdesk.worldbank.org/knowledgebase/articles/906519-world-bank-country-and-lending-groups.

Measuring inequality

The Gini coefficient, a measure of the degree of inequality of a distribution, is a useful tool to measure inequality. On a scale from zero to one, a higher Gini coefficient indicates a larger degree of inequality. In the presence of a high Gini coefficient, high-income households receive a greater percentage of the economy's income. Many developing countries in the world experience high Gini coefficients (Table 9.2).

Global inequality

Global inequality refers to the relative inequality among the world's people, regardless of country of origin. In a historical perspective, two global trends exist. First, global inequality rose from 1820 to 1990. This outcome resulted from divergent growth processes. Developed countries experienced greater gains in income, relative to developing countries. During this period, the average level of inequality within countries was stable or decreasing, especially in the middle decades of the twentieth century, a leveling period. Second, toward the end of the twentieth century to the present, this pattern changed. Average inequality rose within some higher-income countries, but inequality between countries fell. The reason for the change is globalization, an increasing level of economic integration between countries. For higher-income countries, globalization reduces employment in the manufacturing sector, leading to declining living standards for lower-income individuals. At the same time, employment gains occur in the developing world as companies outsource jobs to lower-wage regions. The reality is that gains from globalization are uneven (Ravallion, 2018).

Gender inequality

Another area of inequality in developing countries – gender inequality – bedevils the process of economic development. Gender gaps that favor men with respect to economic opportunity, education, and personal autonomy exist in poorer countries. While all countries exhibit gender inequality to a certain degree, disparities in economics, education, and health tend to be greater in countries with lower levels of income. In developing countries, when gender inequality exists, the status quo establishes a social order that penalizes women. The problem exists because many poorer countries have socio-economic features that establish a belief of favoritism toward men. On average, men experience higher levels of income, employment, and economic opportunity. The elimination of gender inequality requires policy interventions that focus on the rights for women in areas of economic opportunity, educational attainment, the legal system, and political representation. A reduction in gender inequality leads to higher levels of income and opportunity for women (Jayachandran, 2015).

Financial inclusion

An important method to reduce inequality in developing countries is financial inclusion. Financial inclusion establishes economic opportunities for low-income members of society. Specifically, the process includes the methods that increase the availability of financial services. This process exists as a dynamic tool for achieving economic opportunity, employment, and income generation for targeted members of the population. A country increases its level of financial inclusion when it provides financial services to new members of the banking sector. To reduce inequality, the method targets those who are excluded from banking, including low-income households, rural residents, and vulnerable members of society. The result of financial inclusion is the establishment of a link between financial services and households. More members of society are then able to participate in the formal sector. The result is access to financial resources, a rise in living standards, and an increase in the quality of life for low-income households (Omar and Inaba, 2020).

Poverty

Global poverty entails the state of deprivation in which individuals do not have access to the resources and basic necessities to live healthy lives. When people live in poverty, they cannot afford enough food, housing, or medical care. A lack of nutrition causes developmental problems in children. In cities, a lack of access to clean water and sanitation leads to the spreading of preventable diseases, especially among young people. Economists measure poverty in terms of per-capita income: half of the people in the world live on less than $6.85 per day, a measure of global poverty. Extreme poverty, those who live on less than $2.15 per day, includes more than 700 million people, almost one out of every 10 people in the world. While global progress on poverty reduction occurred during the first two decades of this century, the coronavirus pandemic served as a setback. During the pandemic, a global decline in employment and health disproportionately impacted the most vulnerable members of society.

Multidimensional poverty

As a comprehensive measure, the Multidimensional Poverty Index – created in 2010 by the United Nations and Oxford University – includes 10 indicators: assets, child mortality, cooking fuel, drinking water, electricity, housing, nutrition, sanitation, school attendance, and years of schooling. For countries, the report demonstrates poverty profiles, necessary for the implementation of policies that fight the problem. For example, in Niger, the country with the largest level of multidimensional poverty, a low average number of years of schooling, poor nutrition, and low school attendance serve as the largest contributors to the high poverty level. In Botswana, a country with a smaller level of multi-dimensional poverty, low average nutrition, a large number of houses without cooking fuel, and a lack of electricity in many homes exist as the most important indicators. The report finds that, among developing countries, about half of the people who live in multidimensional poverty are under the age of 18 (UNDP and OPHI, 2022).

Vicious cycle

In many developing countries, generational poverty perpetuates low living standards. Known as the **vicious cycle of poverty**, generational poverty includes low incomes, a lack of wealth, food and housing insecurity, a lack of education and healthcare, and little economic opportunity (Figure 9.2). These interrelated factors perpetuate the vicious cycle, preventing families from experiencing rising living standards. Without external intervention, generational poverty often persists. But breaking the cycle entails a comprehensive approach, including the education of all members of society, the growth in employment and economic opportunities, good governance, and other forms of progress. Around the world, the fact that millions of people live in extreme poverty demonstrates the challenge of breaking the vicious cycle of poverty.

Figure 9.2 Vicious cycle of poverty.

Source: Author.

Key terms

Climate change
Economic development
Economic inequality
Formal sector
Informal sector
Microfinance
Value added
Vicious cycle of poverty

Questions

1 For the process of economic development, what is the role of the service sector?
2 With respect to developing countries, what are some common characteristics?
3 In developing countries, why does climate change lead to inequitable outcomes?
4 What are the characteristics of the informal sector?
5 Why do vulnerable members of society experience income inequality?

References

Adenle, Ademola, Ford, James, Morton, John, Twomlow, Stephen, Alverson, Keith, Cattaneo, Andrea, Cervigni, Rafaello, Kurukulasuriya, Pradeep, Huq, Saleemul, Helfgott, Ariella and Ebinger, Jane. 2017. "Managing Climate Change Risks in Africa—A Global Perspective." *Ecological Economics*, 141: 190–201.

Delechat, Corinne and Medina, Leandro. 2020. "What Is the Informal Economy?" *International Monetary Fund*, December. 54–55.

Ebi, Kristie and Hess, Jeremy. 2020. "Health Risks Due to Climate Change: Inequity in Causes and Consequences." *Health Affairs*, 39(12): 2056–2062.

Hsiang, Solomon and Kopp, Robert. 2018. "An Economist's Guide to Climate Change Science." *Journal of Economic Perspectives*, 32(4): 3–32.

Jayachandran, Seema. 2015. "The Roots of Gender Inequality in Developing Countries." *Annual Review of Economics*, 7: 63–88.

La Porta, Rafael and Shleifer, Andrei. 2014. "Informality and Development." *Journal of Economic Perspectives*, 28(3): 109–126.

Omar, Md Abdullah and Inaba, Kazuo. 2020. "Does Financial Inclusion Reduce Poverty and Income Inequality in Developing Countries? A Panel Data Analysis." *Journal of Economic Structures*, 9(37).

Ravallion, Martin. 2018. "Inequality and Globalization: A Review Essay." *Journal of Economic Perspectives*, 56(2): 620–642.

UNDP (United Nations Development Programme) and OPHI (Oxford Poverty and Human Development Initiative). 2022. *Global Multidimensional Poverty Index (MPI): Unpacking Deprivation Bundles to Reduce Multidimensional Poverty*. New York: United Nations.

Part II

Special topics in international economics

10 Global economic shock
The coronavirus pandemic

ESSENTIAL SUMMARY

The coronavirus pandemic (2020–2022) caused widespread disruption to economies. Economists model the macroeconomy with aggregate supply and aggregate demand, demonstrating the behavior of the economy's output (measured with real gross domestic product) and the average price level (measured by a consumer price index). Before the onset of the coronavirus pandemic, many economies in the world were operating at full employment. But the pandemic decreased economic activity. As a result, governments implemented expansionary fiscal policy to stimulate household spending. After inflation rose, governments implemented contractionary monetary policy. At the beginning of the pandemic, the networks of globalization, which include human transmission networks, facilitated the spread of the novel coronavirus.

Global disruption

The coronavirus pandemic (2020–2022) caused widespread economic disruption. While governments implemented policicies to counter economic downturns, the pandemic existed as a **shock**. In economics, a shock occurs when an unexpected and large-scale event disrupts the economy.

External shock

Shocks are either **endogenous** or **exogenous** events. Endogenous shocks originate within an economy. An example is the 2008 financial crisis, which began in the banking system in the United States and spread in a

DOI: 10.4324/9781003434900-12

process of contagion. Exogenous shocks such as the coronavirus pandemic are caused by factors outside of economies. In December 2019, the disease COVID-19 was caused by severe acute respiratory syndrome coronavirus (SARS-CoV-2), the virus responsible for the (SARS-Cov-1) epidemic of 2003. After originating in China, the novel coronavirus of 2020 quickly expanded throughout the world, as infected individuals boarded planes and trains, spreading the virus through human transmission networks. Governments responded by implementing large-scale quarantines, economic shutdowns, and sheltering-in-place requirements. In economies, the coronavirus pandemic initially impacted contact-intensive work in the service sector. But, through economic linkages, it then impacted other areas, including the financial and industrial sectors and global supply chains. The results were severe. Production tumbled. Unemployment rose. Non-essential employees worked remotely.

Inequality of outcomes

The pandemic existed as a "great unequalizer," exposing disparities between income groups. The individuals in lower-income quintiles suffered disproportionately, compared to their higher-income counterparts. Because of pre-existing conditions and less access to medical care, vulnerable individuals were exposed to infections at higher rates than the general population. In effect, the infectious pathogen exploited biological, economic, and social vulnerabilities. Older age groups were more susceptible to COVID-19. But mortality rates that were conditional on age were higher for vulnerable members of the population, especially ethnic and racial minorities. In addition, the inequality of outcomes associated with COVID-19 were due to economic determinants (differences in employment and income), medical determinants (differences in health care insurance and quality), and social determinants (differences in education and health). The fact that COVID-19 disproportionately impacted the lives of the frail and disadvantaged was a function of economic and social dynamics, the characteristics of the pandemic, and differences in the ability of members of the population to protect their health status (Alsan et al., 2021).

Aggregate supply and aggregate demand

Economists use aggregate supply (*AS*) and aggregate demand (*AD*) to model the behavior of the economy's output (measured with real gross domestic product) and the average price level (measured by a consumer price index). The *AD* curve shows the quantity of output demanded at different price levels. The components that contribute to *AD* are elements of gross domestic product: consumption, investment, government spending, and net exports. The *AS* curve shows the total supply of output produced in the economy at different price levels. While the *AD* curve always slopes downward, the shape of *AS* depends on the time horizon.

Long run

The long-run *AS* curve is vertical. In the long run, the price level does not alter the determinants of real GDP. Instead, an economy's output is a function of capital, labor, natural resources, and technology. The long-run aggregate supply (*LRAS*) curve demonstrates monetary neutrality, which applies in the long run, but not for short-run changes in the production of output (Figure 10.1). The equilibrium level of output (Q_e) refers to the economy's potential or natural level. In the long run, the economy moves to this level. But changes in capital, labor, natural resources, and technology cause the *LRAS* curve to shift, resulting in a new natural level of output. For example, an increase in the economy's capital stock raises both the productivity of labor and level of production, shifting *LRAS* to the right, increasing Q_e, and decreasing P_e.

Short run

In the short run, the price level influences the production of output. As a result, the short-run aggregate supply (*SRAS*) curve slopes upward. In the short run, when the price level increases, quantity supplied increases (Figure 10.2). But, similar to the long run, the determinants of *SRAS* are capital, labor, natural resources, and technology. When these variables change, the *SRAS* curve shifts. For example, when

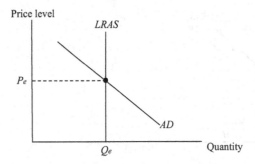

Figure 10.1 Vertical *LRAS* and long-run equilibrium.

Source: Author.

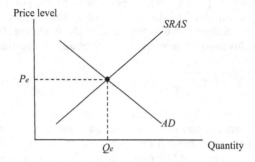

Figure 10.2 Upward-sloping *SRAS* and short-run equilibrium.

Source: Author.

labor force participation declines during a pandemic, *SRAS* shifts to the left. In the short run, *SRAS* is also a function of the expected price level. An increase in the expected price level leads to higher wages, which shifts *SRAS* to the left.

Economic downturn during the pandemic

Before the onset of the coronavirus pandemic, many economies were operating at full employment. But the pandemic led to a decrease in the production of output. To model the pandemic shock, suppose an economy's initial equilibrium position occurs at the natural level of output (point *a* in Figure 10.3). The pandemic shock leads to two effects. On the supply side, sheltering-in-place requirements and supply chain disruptions reduce labor force participation, leading

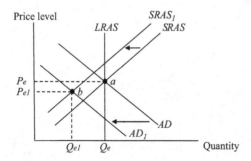

Figure 10.3 Pandemic shock.

Source: Author.

to a decrease in *SRAS* to *SRAS₁*. On the demand side, when businesses send non-essential workers home, the unemployment rate rises and household income falls: *AD* decreases to *AD₁*. The result is a movement to equilibrium point *b*, a decrease in output below the natural rate (Q_{e1}), and a lower price level (P_{e1}). In the model, the magnitude of the shift in *SRAS* is less than the magnitude of the shift in *AD*.

The supply shock and demand shortage

The negative supply shock triggered a demand shortage, leading to a reduction in employment and output that exceeded the size of the supply shock (Guerrieri et al., 2022). The reason is that the forces of aggregate supply and aggregate demand are intertwined. When household income decreased during the pandemic shock, consumption fell, leading to a decrease in aggregate demand. In economies with multiple sectors, the pandemic shock was concentrated, impacting certain sectors more than others. Early in the pandemic, construction, in-person retail, and tourism shut down. During the period of economic shutdown, total spending by households declined. There were two outcomes. First, because some goods and services were no longer available, households had less incentive to spend as much money as they were spending before the pandemic. Second, a shortage of output in specific sectors encouraged households to spend more in other sectors through a process of substitution. For example, households shifted to online entertainment and curbside delivery, rather than going to movies or restaurants. Figure 10.4 demonstrates this process with a two-sector economy. When the pandemic strikes, the first sector is impacted but the second sector is not. The result of the shock is that workers in the first sector stop receiving income, but continue spending on output from the second sector. Overall, the impact on output and employment depended on the

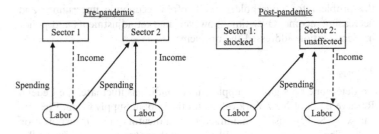

Figure 10.4 Negative supply shock.
Source: Author.

relative strength of these two effects. The decrease in aggregate demand exceeded the decrease in aggregate supply because of low substitutability of spending across sectors (Guerrieri et al., 2022).

Unemployment

In April of 2020, when government interventions led to a decline in economic activity, the unemployment rate rose in countries that did not maintain a link between workers and their employers, including the United States. Many countries in the European Union, in contrast, maintained the link between workers and employers, so the unemployment rate did not rise at the same rate (Table 10.1). For example, in the United States, during 2020, when economic shutdown interventions occurred, the unemployment rate rose from 4.4 percent in March to 14.7 percent in April. But, in the European Union, during the same period, the unemployment rate rose from 6.5 percent to 6.8 percent. The difference involved the regions' methods of addressing the problem of unemployment. While countries in the European Union and the United States eventually implemented generous stimulus packages, sending money directly to businesses and households in response to the pandemic recession, countries in the European Union prioritized the link between workers and their employers. When restrictions eased, workers in the European Union returned to their places of employment, while many workers in the United States remained unemployed.

Market adjustment and policy response

The downturn in economic activity that resulted from the coronavirus pandemic impacted businesses and households. On the supply side, the problem during the initial interval of the pandemic entailed vulnerabilities in the **global supply chain**, the network of companies that produce and distribute goods and services around the world. On the demand side, the problem for households was twofold: economic uncertainty and decreasing income. Over time, however, market adjustments and policy implementation addressed the problems.

The supply side

To determine how global supply-chain conditions fluctuate, the Federal Reserve Bank of New York calculates the Global Supply Chain Pressure Index (GSCPI), using manufacturing indicators and transportation costs. The Fed uses the GSCPI to assess the intensity of global shocks. According to the Fed, a rise in the GSCPI is correlated with goods and producer price inflation, demonstrating how supply-chain inefficiencies

Table 10.1 Unemployment rates in the European Union and United States in 2020

	Jan.	Feb.	Mar.	Apr.	May	Jun.	Jul.	Aug.	Sep.	Oct.	Nov.	Dec.
European Union	6.7	6.6	6.5	6.8	7.0	7.4	7.7	7.8	7.8	7.6	7.4	7.5
United States	3.5	3.5	4.4	14.7	13.2	11.0	10.2	8.4	7.9	6.9	6.7	6.7

Sources: Statista (European Union), https://www.statista.com/statistics/264887/monthly-unemployment-rate-in-the-eu-and-euro-area; Bureau of Labor Statistics (United States), https://data.bls.gov/timeseries/LNS14000000.

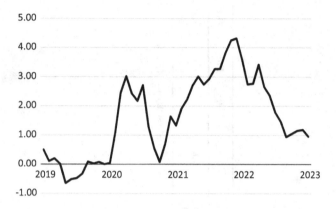

Figure 10.5 Global supply chain pressure index.

Source: Author using data from the Federal Reserve Bank of New York, https://www.newyorkfed.org/research/policy/gscpi#/overview.

link to economic outcomes. In Figure 10.5, global supply-chain pressure is rising in the GSCPI when the index is increasing. Before the pandemic, in 2019, the index was decreasing, thus demonstrating a decline in pressure. During this period, the global supply chain was operating efficiently. In March of 2020, however, the coronavirus pandemic shocked the global economy. Between April and July of 2020, the GSCPI rose, before falling in the later months of the year. During 2021, the index rose again, peaking in December. After that time, the index declined, demonstrating a decreasing level of pressure and a growing level of supply-chain stability.

Before the pandemic began, the global supply chain produced and distributed goods to consumers in an efficient manner. But many firms around the world outsourced elements of their supply chain to outside companies, reducing production costs, storage overheads, and transportation expenditures. As demand varied, manufacturers decreased the quantity of intermediate goods used in production, relying on just-in-time delivery methods. The result was an increase in the efficiency of the system, but a reliance on networks with many interdependent nodes, each vulnerable to an external shock. This level of complexity coupled with the pandemic disruption meant that it took a long time to solve the dual problems of declining production and rising prices, evident in the GSCPI during 2020 and 2021.

During the initial interval of the pandemic, in the second and third quarters of 2020, when global infections were rising and production was falling, several problems persisted. The closing of factories,

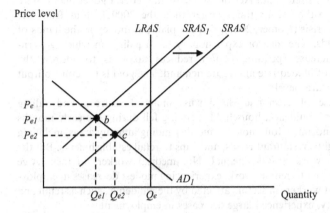

Figure 10.6 Increase in short-run aggregate supply from $SRAS_1$ to $SRAS_2$.
Source: Author.

inefficient distribution in the trucking industry, rising shipping costs, freight delays, and an inability to find a sufficient number of workers to unload goods at ports created the global supply chain disruption. Rising input costs and market shortages led to price increases for construction materials, food, fuel, and many other items. Along with the closing of non-essential businesses, these outcomes led to a decrease in short-run aggregate supply.

But, throughout 2022 and into 2023, the GSCPI declined. The global supply chain stabilized. During this time, factories around the world increased their levels of production. Worker shortages decreased, providing much-needed labor in transportation, especially shipping and trucking. In countries around the world, unemployment fell, labor force participation rose, and economies stabilized. While inflation bedeviled economies throughout 2022 and into 2023, activist monetary policy addressed the problem. In the model, the result of a return of global supply chains to efficient levels of production and distribution was an increase in $SRAS_1$ back to its original position of $SRAS$, a movement from equilibrium point b to c, and a decline in the price level from P_{e1} to P_{e2} (Figure 10.6). The problem was that output was still below the natural level ($Q_{e2} < Q_e$).

The demand side

For many countries, the short-term fiscal responses to the pandemic recession were extensive and swift. In the United States, the

American Rescue Plan Act of 2021 cost the federal government more than $5 trillion, four times larger than the 2009 bailout from the financial crisis (Romer, 2021). But the plan put money in the hands of households. The idea of expansionary **fiscal policy**, in which governments increase spending and/or reduces taxes, is to address the problem of inadequate aggregate demand. The goal is to return output to the natural level.

Because of economic shutdowns, financial distress, and falling consumer confidence, household spending fell during the early months of the pandemic. Households reduced spending in many areas, including plane flights, restaurant meals, and trips to retail establishments. But the effect on workers was unequal. Non-medical workers in the service sector shifted to remote work, experiencing modest decreases in employment. But workers in sectors affected by the pandemic, such as retail and hospitality, experienced large decreases in employment.

The government fiscal packages were intended to counter the decrease in both household spending and business activity. The government responses included expanded unemployment insurance, state and local fiscal relief, and stimulus payments (Romer, 2021). This economic policy successfully mitigated the worst economic problems: falling incomes and rising unemployment. But the countries that implemented large-scale fiscal responses experienced a new risk: they assumed more private-sector and public-sector debt. As time passed, however, it became clear that the fiscal responses were excessive in stimulating production and providing income to households and businesses. The reason was an increase in the inflation rate.

In many countries, before the pandemic, inflation existed at a moderate level with respect to consumer prices. During the early months of the pandemic, inflation decreased, as both aggregate supply and aggregate demand declined. But more than a year after the onset of the pandemic, households had more money than usual after months of saving and repeated stimulus checks from the government. As a result, households started purchasing durable goods, such as automobiles and furniture. This activity led to an increase in prices. At the same time, food prices were rising, while cost increases in services were high in areas such as car repairs and medical care. The inflation data in countries such as the United States demonstrate how the price level – as measured by the Consumer Price Index – remained stable throughout 2020, the first year of the pandemic, but began rising during 2021, the second year, and continued in 2022 (Figure 10.7).

In the model, the increase in aggregate demand (AD_1 to AD_2) from the government stimulus policy moves the equilibrium position from point c to d (Figure 10.8). The cost of the overly-aggressive fiscal policy that creates output Q_{e3}, beyond the natural level, is P_{e3}. While the

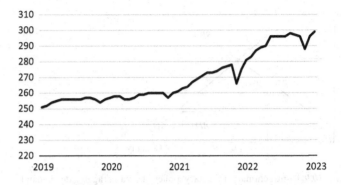

Figure 10.7 Change in the consumer price index in the United States

Source: Author using data from the Bureau of Labor Statistics, https://data.bls.gov/cgi-bin/surveymost.

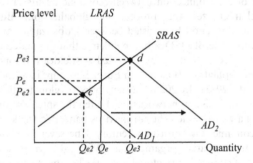

Figure 10.8 Expansionary fiscal policy increases aggregate demand from AD_1 to AD_2.

Source: Author.

unemployment rate declines, a higher price level reduces household purchasing power.

Because high levels of inflation persisted throughout 2021 and 2022, central banks implemented contractionary **monetary policy** by raising interest rates and reducing the money supply. The objectives were to reduce borrowing and decrease the rate of inflation. As interest rates rose and the money supply fell, the contractionary monetary policy lowered household spending, reducing aggregate demand (AD_2 to AD), returning equilibrium to point *a*, decreasing output to the natural level, and lowering the price level to its original position (Figure 10.9).

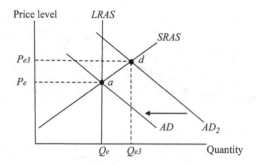

Figure 10.9 Contractionary monetary policy decreases aggregate demand from AD_2 to AD.

Source: Author.

The impact of the pandemic on the global economy

The increasing level of interconnection between economic agents in the global economy characterizes the process of globalization. But, throughout history, a connection has existed between globalization and pandemics. For example, the Black Death, a pandemic that originated in Asia in the 1330s and reached Europe by 1347, led to the death of one-third of the European population. It arrived in Europe on ships in a trade network (Antras et al., 2023). In 2020, the networks of globalization, which include human transmission networks, facilitated the spread of the novel coronavirus on a global scale. The coronavirus pandemic triggered the largest global economic downturn in a century. The severity of the pandemic resulted from spatial organization. When the virus was spreading, the benefit of connection to global networks became a problem of contagion. The individuals who were more connected to the networks of globalization were affected by disease contagion. While flight paths, highways, and shipping lanes facilitated global commerce, they also created pathways for a devastating negative flow: the infectious pathogen.

Contagion

During the coronavirus pandemic, the average incubation period – the time between an infection and the demonstration of symptoms – averaged five days, but individuals could spread the virus two days after exposure. As a result, the pandemic proliferated, leading to more than 800,000 global confirmed cases and 40,000 deaths by March 31, 2020, according to the World Health Organization. By the end of 2020, more than 65,000,000 global confirmed cases and 1,500,000 deaths occurred.

The novel coronavirus affected all human groups and societies, but disproportionately impacted the most vulnerable members of the population. The pandemic led to a rise in inequality within and across societies. The economic effects were particularly disruptive in developing countries where the decrease in income and production exposed economic fragility. Businesses and households already experiencing tenuous circumstances were not equipped to address the severity of the external shock of that duration and scale. On a global scale, the effects were severe. For the first time in a generation, global poverty increased. For workers with a primary education or less, unemployment soared during the initial infection wave. For informal sector businesses that did not have access to credit, the pandemic disrupted market activity.

Eventually, the development and distribution of vaccines coupled with defensive strategies by countries, including quarantines, economic shutdowns, and sheltering-in-place directives, slowed the spread of the virus. By the end of 2022, the pandemic continued to impact societies with confirmed cases and deaths, but methods of adaptation facilitated the return to pre-pandemic levels of economic activity.

Sectors

Capturing the effects of the economic shutdown policies across multiple sectors (primary, secondary, tertiary, quaternary) demonstrates the economic impact of the pandemic. Primary sectors – agriculture, energy, and mining – suffered from lockdown orders and limited worker mobility. A decrease in global energy demand led to a fall in oil consumption. Secondary sectors – construction, manufacturing, and utilities – experienced a decline in demand for their goods and services due to a decrease in economic activity and an increase in economic uncertainty. Because of a decline in services and industry, the demand for electricity and water fell during the period of economic shutdown. Tertiary sectors – finance, healthcare, pharmaceuticals, and retail – suffered from a reduction in the global movement of goods and services in supply chains. However, pharmaceutical companies experienced rising profits due to the development of medications and vaccines. Quaternary sectors – education and research – experienced lower levels of economic activity as students were sent home and workers did not have access to their labs. For countries around the world, educational-related shutdowns created multiple forms of disruption (Delardas et al., 2022).

Key terms

Endogenous
Exogenous

Fiscal policy
Global supply chain
Monetary policy
Shock

Questions

1 Why did the pandemic exist as a "great unequalizer" in terms of its effects on different population groups?
2 How does the aggregate supply/aggregate demand model establish an equilibrium price level and output?
3 How does the aggregate supply/aggregate demand model explain the downturn in economic activity during the initial interval of the pandemic?
4 After the onset of the pandemic, what government policy responses occurred?
5 How did the coronavirus pandemic impact the global economy?

References

Alsan, Marcella, Chandra, Amitabh and Simon, Kosali. 2021. "The Great Unequalizer: Initial Health Effects of Covid-19 in the United States." *Journal of Economic Perspectives*, 35(3): 25–46.

Antras, Pol, Redding, Stephen and Rossi-Hansberg, Esteban. 2023. "Globalization and Pandemics." *American Economic Review*, 113(4): 939–981.

Delardas, Orestis, Kechagias, Konstantinos, Pontikos, Pantelis and Giannos, Panagiotis. 2022. "Socio-Economic Impacts and Challenges of the Coronavirus Pandemic (Covid-19): An Updated Review." *Sustainability*, 14: 9699.

Guerrieri, Veronica, Lorenzoni, Guido, Straub, Ludwig and Werning, Ivan. 2022. "Macroeconomic Implications of Covid-19: Can Negative Supply Shocks Cause Demand Shortages?" *American Economic Review*, 112(5): 1437–1474.

Romer, Christina. 2021. "The Fiscal Policy Response to the Pandemic." *Brookings Papers on Economic Activity*, Spring: 89–110. https://muse.jhu.edu/issue/47251

11 BRICS

The emerging economies of
Brazil, Russia, India, China, and
South Africa

ESSENTIAL SUMMARY

Emerging economies in rapid-growth countries with rising per-capita incomes use economic liberalization as the primary mechanism for growth. As an upper-middle-income country, Brazil has characteristics of high-income countries, including a diverse economy, high literacy rate, skilled workforce, and global economic integration. With upper-middle-income status, Russia experiences a high level of integration into the global economy. With growing global influence, India advocates for developing countries with its interests in agriculture, auto components, banking, and technology. During the first two decades of this century, China had the world's fastest-growing economy. In the mid-1990s, South Africa transitioned to democracy and improved the well-being of its citizens.

Growth in the private sector

Emerging economies in rapid-growth countries with rising per-capita incomes use **economic liberalization** as the primary mechanism for growth. Economic liberalization means both the minimization of government regulations and reliance on market forces. Emerging economies commit to the market mechanism, integrate into the global economy, and encourage private enterprise. But a focus on the private sector leads to important challenges. **Privatization**, the transfer of a firm from public to private ownership, pressures companies to become more efficient. Privatization also leads to interaction with foreign firms. Even though emerging economies are advancing through their processes of economic development, they may have developing-country status. In 2000, China and India were low-income countries, while Brazil, Russia,

DOI: 10.4324/9781003434900-13

Table 11.1 Income classifications and GDP

Country	2000 income classification	2020 income classification	2020 GDP in millions of US $
Brazil	Lower-middle-income	Upper-middle-income	1,608,981
Russia	Lower-middle-income	Upper-middle-income	1,778,782
India	Low-income	Lower-middle-income	3,176,295
China	Low-income	Upper-middle-income	17,734,062
South Africa	Lower-middle-income	Upper-middle-income	419,015

Sources: Hoskisson et al. (2000) and the World Bank, https://datahelpdesk.worldbank.org/knowledgebase/articles

and South Africa were lower-middle-income countries (Table 11.1). By 2020, all of these countries advanced to higher income classifications.

International business

In emerging economies, **multinational enterprises** (MNEs) serve as important institutions. They establish a link between developed countries and emerging economies. They transmit capital, knowledge, technology, and values across country borders. They extend production opportunities into the global economy. In addition, MNEs facilitate a majority of the world's foreign direct investment (FDI), the latter being the establishment of an ownership stake in a foreign company. In emerging economies, the MNEs undertake FDI through the choice of strategic locations, entry strategies, and creation of international trade opportunities. Positive spillover effects from MNEs include better business reputations and market share. Negative spillover effects lead to adverse reactions from stakeholders with respect to employment, labor practices, and pollution. The recognition of both positive and negative interests helps to identify outcomes that impact businesses, host countries, and stakeholders (Meyer, 2004).

Outward flow of FDI

Foreign direct investment also flows from emerging economies to the rest of the world. Many businesses from Brazil, Russia, India, China, and South Africa contribute to global production networks. This outward flow of FDI results from trade liberalization. Changes in both foreign trade and investment practices have inspired businesses in emerging economies to seek foreign markets. In general, FDI is a function of four interconnected motivations: efficiency-seeking, market-seeking, resource-seeking, and strategic asset-seeking. These motivations exist for businesses with an international focus.

Business strategies

In emerging economies, economic transformation impacts business strategies. The reason is that high-income economies have stronger economic, government, and social institutions. In emerging economies, these institutions are in the process of development. But, as markets integrate into the global economy, three areas of focus become important: institutional theory, resource allocation, and transaction costs.

Institutional theory

Business organizations operate in an economic system. The system influences the process of decision making. Not only do businesses respond to market incentives and regulatory forces, but they also respond to internal capabilities, economic opportunities, and macro-social forces. Market incentives encourage constrained optimization. Regulation oversees business activity. Internal capabilities determine the level of new production technology. Economic opportunities incentivize cost minimization. Macro social forces make businesses aware of society's concerns. Together, these factors demonstrate that business strategy includes profit maximization, external and internal influences, and an emphasis on efficiency (Sadler, 2006).

Resource allocation

Businesses have heterogeneous economic resources. But the resources differ with respect to their applications, so resource value determines competitive advantage. Overall, firms establish **institutional capital** – the capacity for action and speed of decision making – to enhance their productive capabilities. In emerging economies, first mover advantages exist for companies that create value in growing markets. The advantages include being the first to offer new products, establish reputational effects, and create economies of scale. These advantages, however, require embeddedness in the marketplace. This embeddedness creates access to labor and product markets, transportation networks, and systems of distribution (Hoskisson et al., 2000).

Transaction costs

In the marketplace, businesses assume the costs of individual transactions. For example, they determine which components to produce inside the company, co-produce, or outsource. The objective is to establish contractual relationships that create value while at the same time avoiding waste. To make the best decisions in emerging markets, companies establish optimal forms of organization to match the characteristics of business transactions. Recurring but risky transactions occur through vertical forms of integration. Less common but safe transactions occur through co-producing contracts. Fungible forms of business activity occur through outsourcing. At the margin, the choice of business organization creates a tradeoff between transaction costs and the degree of control. In emerging economies, as capital and labor markets develop, diversification within the business organization occurs.

Brazil

As an upper-middle-income country, Brazil has many characteristics of high-income countries, including a diverse economy, high literacy rate, skilled workforce, and global integration. But the coronavirus pandemic saddled Brazil with a large death toll. An effective vaccine program coupled with economic support contributed to a slow but steady return to pre-pandemic levels of economic activity. After the pandemic, GDP growth, a decrease in unemployment, and a labor market recovery fueled the process of recovery. Brazil also experiences problems that are common among lower-income countries, including food insecurity, income inequality, and poverty, although federal systems of social support exist. Government inefficiencies, fueled by corruption, mismanagement, and turmoil, have hampered the ability of the country to maintain a stable level of GDP per capita (Figure 11.1). A government fiscal deficit and a labor force participation rate that is below other upper-middle-income countries also play important roles.

Economic integration

Brazil traces its integration into the global economy to the internationalization of domestic enterprises in the 1970s. But the liberalization of both investment and trade, in the 1990s, integrated businesses into foreign markets (Bezuidenhout et al., 2021). While a substantial amount of the country's economic exchange occurs with the trade agreement of Mercosur, the European Union, and the United States, Brazil also trades with African and Asian countries, including Nigeria, Angola, Algeria, South Africa, and China. Brazil's trade with China, in fact, is a structural part of the economy. Since the beginning of this century, China developed into Brazil's main trading partner. In a majority of Brazil's 26 states, China serves as the primary destination for exports. Brazil sends soy, iron ore, and oil to China, while importing semiconductors, office machine parts, and cell phones from China.

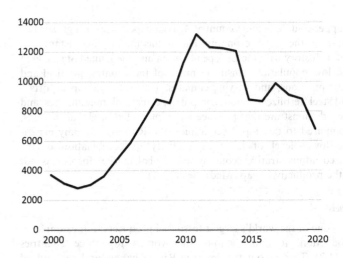

Figure 11.1 Brazil's GDP per capita in US dollars.

Source: Author using data from Data Commons, https://datacommons.org/place/country/BRA.

Environmental outcomes

In the global economy, Brazil exists as a leading agricultural exporter, seeking to expand markets for its agricultural products. But importers have expressed concern about the products that result from **deforestation**, the act of clearing large tracts of trees for the purpose of economic gain. Although most of Brazil's agricultural exports do not result from deforestation, the process occurs in the Amazonian region, which is a tropical rainforest. When deforestation occurs, the carbon stored in trees flows back into the atmosphere in the form of carbon dioxide, contributing to the problem of climate change. The reason that deforestation occurs in Brazil is to clear land for cattle and crops. The world's increasing demand for beef, corn, soybeans, and sugarcane incentivizes Brazilian cattle ranchers and farmers to cut down sections of the rainforest. From an environmental perspective, Brazil's trading partners that import goods from deforested processes are complicit in promoting deforestation. To solve the problem, Brazil must strengthen its systems of environmental enforcement, forest monitoring, and mapping. But the global demand for Brazil's exports remains a roadblock (Rajao et al., 2020).

Russia

As an upper-middle-income country, Russia experiences a high level of integration in the global economy. Russia has unique circumstances in terms of its history with the European Union and the United States, long borders, low population density in much of the country, political and economic positions, and varying climates. The country's top exports – iron and steel, fertilizers, wood, computers, cereals, aluminum, ores, and plastics – demonstrate that producers are integrated in global markets. But, compared to developed economies, the Russian economy experiences a lower level of labor productivity. A combination of the centralized administrative economy and global market forces has not closed the productivity gap (Medvedev, 2015).

Fossil fuels

Russia is one of the world's largest fossil fuel producers. For example, in oil production, it ranks among the world's top three countries (Table 11.2). Throughout the country, Russia has natural gas and oil facilities. But most of the fields exist in Siberia. Several important outcomes result from the high level of fossil fuel production. First, in global energy markets, Russia serves as a major exporter. The actions it takes to alter its supply of fossil fuels have global ramifications. Second, Russia relies on the revenue it generates from both natural gas and oil exports to contribute to the federal budget. Third, Russia has an extensive network of fossil fuel pipelines, which allows the country to export large volumes to both Asia and Europe. Fourth, because of its large level of refining capacity, Russia produces many oil products, including diesel and gasoline.

Table 11.2 World's top oil producers in 2022

Country	Million barrels per day	Share of world total (%)
United States	20.21	20
Saudi Arabia	12.14	12
Russia	10.94	11
Canada	5.70	6
China	5.12	5
Iraq	4.55	5
United Arab Emirates	4.24	4
Brazil	3.77	4
Iran	3.66	4
Kuwait	3.02	3

Source: US Energy Information Administration, https://www.eia.gov/tools/faqs/faq.php?id=709&t=6.

War in Ukraine

On February 24, 2022, Russia invaded and occupied territory in Ukraine, escalating the Ukrainian-Russian conflict that began in 2014. In addition to deaths and the disruption to civilian life, the conflict created negative economic outcomes. First, Russia is the world's second-largest natural gas producer, behind the United States, but it has the world's largest natural gas reserves. The country has been an exporter to the European Union, where natural gas is used for household heating, industrial processes, and power generation. Before the invasion, the European Union imported more than 50 percent of its natural gas from Russia; however, the objective of energy diversification after the invasion led to the European Union importing less than 15 percent of its natural gas from Russia. Second, the conflict led to a decrease in Russian GDP, an increase in economic vulnerability, and **economic sanctions** – the withdrawal of financial and trade arrangements – from the European Union and the United States. The sanctions were large with respect to their breadth, global coordination, and speed, covering defense, energy, financial, and technology sectors. Third, the conflict led to a rising level of tension between Russia and the United States. After the invasion, the United States committed military hardware and intelligence for the restoration of Ukraine's sovereignty, punishing Russia for its military offensive.

India

With a growing level of influence on a global scale, India advocates for developing countries with its interests in agriculture, auto components, banking, and technology. India has resisted efforts that force developing countries to open their economies (Hopewell, 2015). In 2023, India passed China to become the world's largest country with a population of over 1.4 billion people. In many ways, the process of globalization has impacted India's economy. An influx of foreign companies and foreign direct investment leads to technological advances. In the financial sector, innovation and market competition create a dynamic economic environment. Globalization presents opportunities for economic growth, including access to markets and workers, although the benefits of economic integration are not evenly shared. Relative to other countries, India experiences a high level of inequality.

Labor force

For decades, India implemented family planning programs; however, the country experienced varying degrees of success, as many members of the population have little or no education or ties to the formal sector. In the 1990s, policies of economic liberalization led to a growing valuation of the country's young workforce as a demographic dividend. While the country's birth rate has declined, India has the world's largest working-age population of over one billion people. With this young workforce, both benefits and costs exist. One benefit is that industries such as biotechnology and finance, which require educated professionals, grow along with the labor force. Another benefit is that global companies are attracted to India because of its young labor supply, especially in business services. Many of the country's young workers find employment when companies in other countries outsource part of their production processes to India. But, for young members of the labor force to prosper, the economy must create a large number of well-paying jobs on an annual basis. In addition, a young workforce puts pressure on the country to enhance its social services, improve its safety net, and increase educational opportunities for all members of the population, even individuals in lower castes.

Technology and services hub

As global companies enhance their technological capabilities and outsource aspects of production, they are engaging with India as a technology and services hub. Since the beginning of this century, India's technology and service sectors have become more integrated into the global economy, especially in business process outsourcing and information technology. Many international businesses employ Indian workers in global capability centers, which help companies scale their divisions on a global scale. These centers provide workers and technology that support different business functions, including call centers and information technology infrastructures. For companies around the world, the idea is to use talent in India's workforce to support analytics, automation, innovation, and other areas of production. By employing these workers, global companies manage customer inquiries and evolving business practices.

China

During the first two decades of this century, China had the world's fastest-growing economy (Bezuidenhout et al., 2021). The growth of China on the world stage resulted from the country's establishment of an export-oriented economy, growth in the manufacturing sector, and flow of outward FDI through bilateral agreements between China and other countries. With its export orientation, the Chinese economy has altered the composition of its economy over time, moving from the production of less sophisticated forms of output to more sophisticated goods in manufacturing. During this century, the economy experienced a decline in the share of agriculture, apparel, and textiles, but a rise in the share of appliances, computers, electronics, and machinery.

Trade strategy

During China's period of economic growth, the country had a chance to focus on the production of value-added products or the assembly of duty-free forms of output. With the former strategy, production is enhanced with additional market qualities that increase its price above the value of its economic resources. With the latter strategy, an economy assembles commodities that are produced in other countries. For example, Apple assembles many of its iPhones in China, but the components come from companies throughout the world. Overall, much of the growth in exports in China follows the same pattern as the iPhone: the assembly of duty-free forms of imported inputs, which is referred to as processing trade (Amiti and Freund, 2010). The reason is that an important component of the growth in the manufacturing has been the proliferation of duty-free inputs of high-tech content. The country's quest for assets, competitive mechanisms, and markets has led to both inward and outward FDI, the latter including mergers and acquisitions in developing countries. China is diversifying its comparative advantage in manufacturing, specializing in production that requires a mix of capital and labor. By the third decade of this century, the highest dollar value of Chinese exports included electrical machinery, computers, vehicles, plastics, furniture, toys and games, organic chemicals, clothing and accessories, and iron and steel. This list accounted for two-thirds of the overall value of Chinese exports.

Trade war with the United States

In 2018, the United States and China implemented import tariffs against each other, creating a US-China trade war. After the United States imposed import tariffs on Chinese aluminum and steel, China responded with tariffs on US aluminum, fruit, meat, and wine. Over time, the trade war intensified with the implementation of additional trade barriers. The reasons for the trade war were fourfold: to battle for global influence, reduce the countries' economic interdependence, diversify imports, and increase the efficiency of supply chains. By complicating the process of trade, the barriers reduced the ability of domestic businesses to maintain export markets in the other country. The result of the trade war was a reduction in many sectoral imports (Itakura, 2020). For example, four years after the start of the trade war, US imports from China decreased, including clothing, electronics, footwear, furniture, information technology hardware, and semiconductors. But, during the same period of time, other US imports from China increased, including computer monitors, laptops, phones, toys, and video game consoles (Brown, 2022). An important reason for the latter trend was that consumer demand surged during the coronavirus pandemic when households that were sheltering-in-place adjusted their spending toward these Chinese products. The evidence demonstrates that trade wars do not always achieve their objectives.

South Africa

In the mid-1990s, South Africa transitioned to democracy. Since then, the country has improved the well-being of its citizens; however, several challenges exist. For an upper-middle-income country, a significant percentage of the population lives below the poverty line. Electricity shortages plague the country, especially in rural areas. A persistently high unemployment rate for younger members of the labor force limits the economy's growth potential. A high level of income and wealth inequality results from generations of economic exclusion. The outcome is a low level of intergenerational mobility. In this economic context, it is difficult for an individual growing up in a poor household to rise to a higher income class. The economy is exposed to volatility in both capital flows and external shocks. Growing public debt limits the ability of the government to address the country's shortcomings. Labor and product market rigidities reduce the economy's productive capacity. One way the country addresses these challenges is through a growing level of access to education. Investments in early schooling lead to better economic, health, and social outcomes. They also decrease the rate of intergenerational poverty. Another way the country addresses its problems is through economic diversification. South Africa possesses a strong external asset position, robust financial market, and active monetary policy. Together, these factors establish a mixed economic position.

Benefits and costs of exports

Exports serve as an important part of South Africa's economy. The top exports of platinum, gold, iron ore, diamonds, and coal briquettes generate billions of dollars in revenue on an annual basis. The problem is that large companies dominate the export industry, especially in food, fuels, ores, metals, chemicals, textiles, and industrial machinery. The implication is that the income generated from these exports does not benefit everyone. In addition, South Africa does not exploit all of its export markets, compared to Brazil, India, and China. Finally, the diamond and gold markets lead to environmental degradation, illegal elements, labor exploitation, and pollution flows.

Structural reforms

To establish a stable rate of economic growth, the South African economy requires several structural reforms, according to the International Monetary Fund. First, private sector participation in energy markets would enhance energy security. Second, a reduction in carbon intensity would help the country reduce carbon dioxide emissions and reach climate goals. Third, the alleviation of transportation problems would improve logistics. Fourth, efficiency gains for state-owned enterprises would improve the public budget. Fifth, a greater level of trade integration would enhance market competition. Sixth, labor market reforms, including collective bargaining and employment protections, would address the problem of underemployment. Seventh, better governance would increase transparency and reduce corruption. Finally, reducing gender disparities would increase opportunities for marginalized members of the population.

Key terms

Deforestation
Economic liberalization
Economic sanctions
Emerging economies
Institutional capital
Multinational enterprises
Privatization

Questions

1 What are the characteristics of emerging economies?
2 Why does deforestation serve as a problem for some of Brazil's agricultural exports?
3 For Russia, do fossil fuels exist as an important export? Explain.
4 In India, what is the role of the technology and services hub?
5 What is China's trade strategy?

References

Amiti, Mary and Freund, Caroline. 2010. "The Anatomy of China's Export Growth." In Feenstra, Robert and Wei, Shang-Jin (Eds.), *China's Growing Role in World Trade*. Chicago: University of Chicago Press. 35–62.

Bezuidenhout, Henri, Mhonyera, Gabriel, Van Rensburg, Jacob, Sheng, Hsia, Carrera, Jose and Cui, Xinjian. 2021. "Emerging Market Global Players: The Case of Brazil, China and South Africa." *Sustainability*, 13(21): 12234.

Brown, Chad. 2022. "Four Years into the Trade War, Are the US and China Decoupling?" *Peterson Institute for International Economics*, October 20.

Hopewell, Kristen. 2015. "Different Paths to Power: The Rise of Brazil, India and China at the World Trade Organization." *Review of International Political Economy*, 22(2): 311–338.

Hoskisson, Robert, Eden, Lorraine, Lau, Chung and Wright, Mike. 2000. "Strategy in Emerging Economies." *The Academy of Management Journal*, 43(3): 249–267.

Itakura, Ken. 2020. "Evaluating the Impact of the US-China Trade War." *Asian Economic Policy Review*, 15: 77–93.

Medvedev, Dmitry. 2015. "A New Reality: Russia and Global Challenges." *Russian Journal of Economics*, 1(2): 109–129.

Meyer, Klaus. 2004. "Perspectives on Multinational Enterprises in Emerging Economies." *Journal of International Business Studies*, 35: 259–276.

Rajao, Raoni, Soares-Filho, Britaldo, Nunes, Felipe, Borner, Jan, Machado, Lilian, Assis, Debora, Oliveira, Amanda, Pinto, Luis, Ribeiro, Vivian, Rausch, Lisa, Gibbs, Holly and Figueira, Danilo. 2020. "The Rotten Apples of Brazil's Agribusiness." *Science*, 369(6501): 246–248.

Sadler, Thomas R. 2006. "Contemporary Environmental Policy: The Need for an Economics and Management Approach." *The Journal of Interdisciplinary Economics*, 17: 351–377.

12 Brexit

Britain exits the European Union

ESSENTIAL SUMMARY

In the modern era, the Brexit decision serves as the largest reversal of economic integration between countries in a trade agreement. The relationship between the UK and EU did not officially change until the beginning of 2021, when the UK and EU implemented a new Trade and Cooperation Agreement. The agreement established both quota-free and tariff-free exchange between the UK and EU, but it excluded the UK from the EU's Customs Union and Single Market. The Brexit vote impacted the UK's currency value, immigration, inflation, production, trade, and unemployment.

Exiting the European Union

The United Kingdom (UK) exited the European Union (EU) on January 31, 2020. But the UK voted to leave the EU on June 23, 2016. In 2016, the Leave vote established a popular mandate for the UK, increasing the UK's sovereignty over its trade policy; however, Brexit increased the level of future economic uncertainty, according to the Brexit Uncertainty Index. The Index showed the percentage of businesses that reported that Brexit served as a top-three source of economic uncertainty (Figure 12.1). In late 2018 and early 2019, the Index rose above 50 percent with the upcoming withdrawal of the UK. Rising economic uncertainty related to the fact that it was not clear how Brexit would impact the UK's rate of economic growth, employment, or trade. But, even before the exit occurred, the Leave vote altered the flow of investment, exchange rate, and economic activity. In the modern era, the Brexit decision served as the largest reversal of economic integration between countries in a trade agreement (Dhingra and Sampson, 2022).

DOI: 10.4324/9781003434900-14

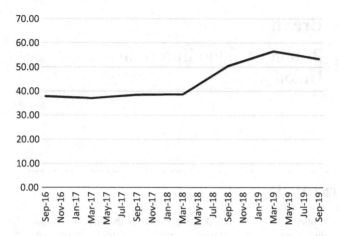

Figure 12.1 Brexit Uncertainty Index, percentage.

Source: Author using data from the Bank of England, https://www.bankofengland.
co.uk/statistics.

Control

Membership in the EU's Single Market means that labor may move freely
between countries in the trade agreement. Membership in the Customs
Union means the EU has jurisdiction over trade policy. The trade
agreement establishes both environmental and labor standards. But
supporters of the Leave position in the UK prioritized domestic **sovereignty**, formal juridical independence. When the Brexit vote occurred,
51.9 percent voted in favor of leaving the EU (Dhingra and Sampson,
2022). But sovereign decision making created new constraints. External
factors impacted domestic outcomes. In the foreign exchange market, the
pound decreased in value. Foreign companies reduced their level of
investment into the UK. A tradeoff existed between local sovereignty
and external openness. The UK relied on exchange with its trading
partners but experienced fewer options for trade as a non-member of the
EU. Effective sovereignty depended as much on economic, political, and
social interactions with foreign countries, companies, and individuals as
it did on domestic decision making (Bryant, 2018).

Shock

Trade agreements decrease trade barriers and increase economic
exchange. But Brexit had the opposite effect, existing as a large shock
to the UK's economy. After the Leave vote, the relationship between

the UK and EU did not immediately change. But the referendum failed to establish a blueprint for future economic activity. After the vote, exchange between the UK and EU became more uncertain. The value of the pound fell, consistent with an expectation of a long-term decline in the return to UK production. An increase in the price of imported inputs led to lower real wages and higher supply chain costs. Importers of UK products were concerned that supply chains would suffer from border delays. Anticipated future trade barriers affected firm behavior. In advance of the actual withdrawal from the EU, domestic supply adjusted. British manufacturing exporters lost business. Commercial service exports declined. Output prices rose. Uncertainty over the withdrawal from the EU harmed business investment, led to higher import costs, and increased the rate of inflation.

New trade arrangement

As a member of the EU from 1973 to 2020, the UK is the only sovereign country to leave the trade agreement. Because of the British exit, the Court of Justice of the European Union does not have governing jurisdiction over British trade laws, with the exception of some areas in Northern Ireland. While the UK left the EU at the beginning of 2020, the economic arrangements between the UK and EU did not officially change until January 1, 2021, when the UK and EU established a new Trade and Cooperation Agreement (TCA).

Characteristics of the TCA

The TCA established both quota-free and tariff-free exchange between the UK and EU; however, it created non-tariff barriers, including border controls, customs checks, health inspections, import duties, and restrictions on business visits. For the UK, the TCA reduced economic integration and market access. In addition, the TCA did not include the UK as a member of the EU's Customs Union or Single Market. The implication was that the TCA established customs and regulatory borders for UK's exporters (Dhingra and Sampson, 2022). To participate in the TCA's quota-free and tariff-free framework of exchange, output produced in the UK had to meet a specific requirement: a majority of the share of the product's value had to originate in the UK or EU. But not all output qualified, so compliance costs sometimes exceeded the tariff savings from following the rules. As a result, trade under the TCA did not always exist in a tariff-free manner. During the first year of the TCA, EU importers paid tariffs on 30 percent of UK exports, instead of benefitting from a zero-tariff policy (Freeman et al., 2022).

Industry example

In Scotland, fishing represents a stable flow of revenue for fishing companies, who export a large percentage of their catch to France and Spain. Before the TCA, the companies would ship their catch by boat and truck in an unimpeded process of distribution. But the TCA reduced the efficiency of the supply chain: exporters had to process an extensive amount of paperwork. They experienced extra checkpoints at the EU border. For the UK, the fishing sector exists as an anomaly. As an island country, it imports much of its seafood, especially the cod used for fish and chips. But the fish that it catches, including crab and lobster, is exported. In general, the TCA complicates this exchange because the market values fresh fish. Boats and trucks crossing into the EU must provide a detailed list of inventory. For exporters, the higher administrative workload increases variable costs. Customs agents may reject the delivery of fish at the border because of inadequate paperwork. Relative to the time before the TCA, the market outcome is more uncertain with respect to supply-side conditions, higher prices, and distribution. In the TCA era, the fish exporters experience the greatest burden (Castle, 2023).

Economic effects

Trade flows are a function of supply conditions in exporting countries, demand conditions in importing countries, and the degree of openness to economic integration among trading partners. The Brexit vote affected the UK's exchange rate, flow of investment, manufacturing sector, and service sector. For UK businesses and foreign firms that used the UK as an economic base, the new economic arrangement led to trade barriers. The economic effects were widespread, including changes to the currency value, immigration, inflation, production, trade, and unemployment. To establish a framework of analysis, three time periods demonstrate changing economic conditions, signified with dotted lines in the figures in the following sections (Freeman et al., 2022):

- Period 1: before the Brexit vote (2000 – June 2016)
- Period 2: between the Brexit vote and TCA (July 2016 – December 2020)
- Period 3: after the implementation of the TCA (January 2021 – December 2022)

Currency

An exchange rate is the price of one currency in terms of another currency. When economic agents buy a home currency, it increases in value (appreciates). When economic agents sell a home currency, it decreases in value (depreciates). For countries, changes in currency values are important because they affect trade flows. When a home currency depreciates, domestic products become less expensive for foreign purchasers, so home-country exports increase. When a home currency appreciates, domestic products become more expensive for foreign purchasers, so home-country exports decrease.

The foreign exchange market determines currency values. Economic agents and organizations involved in international trade participate in this market, including businesses importing goods and travelers purchasing foreign exchange. The supply of British pounds is a function of EU exports to the UK, monetary policy of the British Central Bank, and other factors. If the EU increases its exports to the UK or the UK Central Bank increases its money supply, the supply of pounds increases in the marketplace and the value of the pound decreases. On the demand side, economic agents in the EU who want to import products from the UK purchase British pounds. Among other factors, a shift in demand for British pounds is a function of changing demand for UK output, the inflation rate, and interest rates. If economic agents in the EU demand more output from the UK, the UK's inflation rate decreases, interest rates increase, the demand for pounds rises, and the value of the pound increases.

In Period 1, the value of the pound remained relatively stable, rising before the Brexit vote in 2015 and reaching a high of 1 pound = 1.41 euros on March 11, 2015 (Figure 12.2). But a decrease in the value of the pound started before changes in the UK/EU trade arrangement became official. Brexit served as an important factor in the process. Immediately after the Brexit referendum, the pound experienced its largest single-day drop in 30 years on June 24, 2016.

In Period 2, two substantial decreases in the value of the pound occurred in 2017 and 2019. By 2020, before the implementation of the Trade and Cooperation Agreement, the pound was 15 percent weaker compared to its high in 2015. The reasons for this decline were higher levels of economic uncertainty, negative future expectations, the UK's political instability, and the rise in trade friction between the UK and EU. These factors caused financial institutions to decrease their preferences to hold pound-denominated financial assets. The institutions forecasted lower rates of return. They sold the pound, decreasing its value relative to the euro and other currencies.

In Period 3, the pound remained relatively stable, fluctuating in value between a low of 1.103 euros and a high of 1.208 euros. But, by the end of 2022, a decline in the value of the pound reflected the lasting effects of Brexit, labor market conditions, and tax policy. Overall, a decline in the ability of the UK's economy to fill open positions created labor shortages, especially in healthcare and hospitality. Sluggish economic

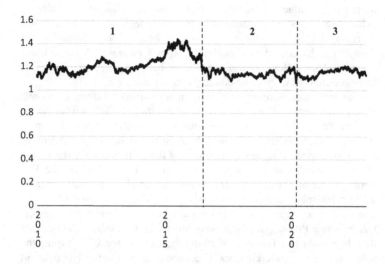

Figure 12.2 €/£ exchange rate: number of euros per British pound.

Source: Author using data from the *Wall Street Journal*, https://www.wsj.com/market-data/quotes/fx/GBPEUR/historical-prices.

growth and rising wages created conditions for a higher inflation rate, which decreased household purchasing power and weakened the pound.

Immigration

A **migrant** is an individual who moves from a home country to another country for their residence. Migration may occur voluntarily or involuntarily. Individuals migrate for economic reasons, looking for employment opportunities, better labor standards, or higher wages. Individuals migrate for social reasons, choosing to study or live near family. Individuals migrate for humanitarian reasons, moving away from conflict, human rights violations, persecution, or terrorism. Individuals migrate for environmental reasons, fleeing from the effects of climate change or natural disasters. In different ways, countries react to the flow of immigrants, including asylum policies, migration routes, and residency and work permits.

In Period 1 before the Brexit vote, from 2000 to June 2016, immigration into the UK from countries around the world varied annually between 479,000 and 680,000 (Figure 12.3). Many of these individuals filled both high-skilled and low-skilled jobs, contributing to a steady unemployment rate between 2000 and 2010, a rising unemployment rate between 2009 and 2013, and a declining rate after 2013. Other immigrants arriving in

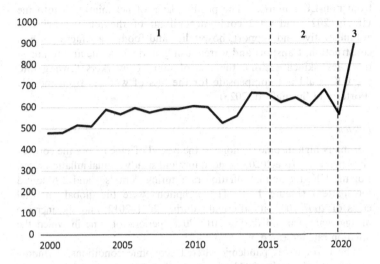

Figure 12.3 Immigration into the United Kingdom in thousands.

Source: Author using data from the House of Commons Library, https://commonslibrary.parliament.uk/research-briefings/sn06077/#:~:text=There%20are%20fewer%20foreign%20nationals,population%20is%20concentrated%20in%20London.

the UK came to study, flee conflict, or reunite with families. Since the beginning of the century, the number of individuals emigrating out of the UK has been less than the number of individuals immigrating into the UK. The net positive flow of migration contributed to growth in the overall population.

In Period 2, after the Leave vote, from July 2016 to December 2020, annual immigration fluctuated between a high of 681,000 in 2019 and low of 563,000 in 2020. The low corresponded with the first year of the pandemic, when international travel declined.

In Period 3, from January 2021 to December 2022, the Trade and Cooperation Agreement eliminated the free movement of workers from the EU to the UK. But, for three reasons, immigration increased, reflecting the unique factors present at the time. First, the world was recovering from the pandemic and travel increased. Second, the UK implemented a relatively liberal immigration system following the withdrawal from the EU. Third, the UK opened its borders for Ukrainian nationals in 2022 following the Russian invasion of Ukraine.

The problem was that, during Period 3, the UK's exit from the EU led to overall labor shortages. During the period, immigration decreased into the UK from EU countries, but immigration increased from non-EU countries. The positive level of net migration into the UK in 2021 and 2022 could not fill all of the job vacancies in administrative and support, hospitality and food, manufacturing and construction, transport and warehousing, and wholesale and retail. In these less-skilled sectors, the rise of non-EU workers flowing into the UK could not compensate for the loss of workers from the EU (Portes and Springford, 2023).

Inflation

For many high-income economies, the period of time before the coronavirus pandemic (pre-2020) included low and steady annual inflation rates. For the UK, the annual inflation rate during Periods 1 and 2 followed this pattern (Figure 12.4). The exceptions were the global financial crisis of 2007–2008, its aftermath during 2011–2012, and the increase in aggregate demand during 2017–2018, periods of time in which the inflation rate increased.

The coronavirus pandemic altered economic conditions, including the price level. During 2020, the pandemic led to a major global supply shock. Supply chain disruptions from problems in manufacturing and distribution led to a decrease in aggregate supply. In 2021, the reopening of economies after the pandemic's initial infection waves led to an

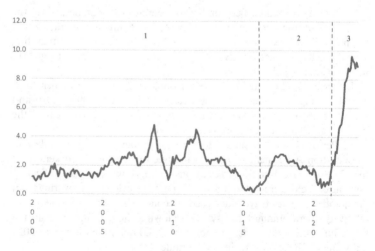

Figure 12.4 United Kingdom consumer price inflation, percentage.

Source: Author using data from the Office for National Statistics, https://www.ons.gov.uk/economy/inflationandpriceindices/timeseries/l55o/mm23.

increase in aggregate demand. Energy and food price increases after Russia's invasion of Ukraine occurred in February 2022.

But, relative to countries in the EU, the UK experienced a higher annual rate of inflation, starting in April 2021. This outcome, occurring in Period 3, led to a rise in the cost of living for UK households. For comparison, during the second quarter of 2022, the UK's inflation rate was 2.8 percent higher than in France, 1.6 percent higher than in Germany, and 3.4 percent higher than in Italy (Posen and Rengifo-Keller, 2022).

Given the pandemic shock to the economies in these countries, what accounted for the higher rate of inflation in the UK? Brexit served as the primary reason. By reducing the movement of workers from the EU to the UK, the UK's labor supply contracted, tightening the labor market. Businesses in the UK could not rely on inexpensive workers from the continent to satisfy labor demand. In the presence of new trade barriers, the UK's household purchasing power declined. The UK's weak currency increased import costs, creating an increase in the cost of imported products. With a rise in economic uncertainty, the withdrawal from the EU raised inflation expectations (Posen and Rengifo-Keller, 2022; Tarr, 2022).

Production

Gross domestic product (GDP) measures the value of final output produced in an economy in a given year. Business cycles demonstrate that GDP rises during periods of economic expansion with higher levels of production but falls during recessions with lower levels of production. During the global financial crisis of 2007–2008, a downturn in the housing market and banking system in the United States spread through a process of contagion to the rest of the world. Production declined, unemployment rose, and millions of people lost their jobs. For many countries, including the UK, the result was a dip in GDP between 2008 and 2009 (Figure 12.5). In 2009, GDP reached a **trough**, the lowest point in the business cycle. This trough occurred during Period 1.

After 2009, the UK's economy experienced a stable period of expansion. The country's GDP rose every year in a continuous process until 2019, when GDP reached a **peak**, the highest point in the business cycle. This peak occurred in Period 2. In 2020, before the implementation of the Trade and Cooperation Agreement between the UK and EU, GDP reached another trough, signaling the end of the expansionary period. During this time, declining incomes and rising unemployment led to a decrease in the demand for imports; however, production in non-tradable forms of economic activity, such as construction, food provision, and healthcare, fell by as much or more than tradable forms of economic activity, such as agricultural production or manufactured goods.

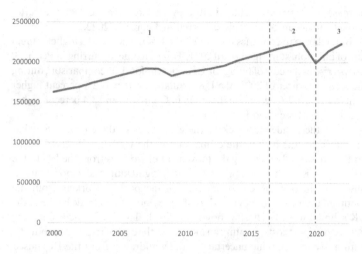

Figure 12.5 United Kingdom GDP in chained volume measures, seasonally adjusted, £ millions.

Source: Author using data from the Office for National Statistics, https://www.ons.gov.uk/economy/grossdomesticproductgdp/timeseries/abmi/pn2.

The Brexit vote had an important effect on GDP. In the period between the UK referendum in June 2016 and the trough of 2020, GDP growth remained positive. But the rate of growth declined. Relative to other Organization for Economic Cooperation and Development (OECD) countries, such as France and Germany, the UK went from having the highest GDP growth rate to the lowest growth rate. This result suggested that international economic trends impacted the UK's GDP, while internal economic trends became weaker. In addition, the UK's labor productivity decreased. After the Brexit vote, the gap in output per worker in the UK and OECD countries widened (De Lyon and Dhingra, 2019).

In Period 3, while the withdrawal of the UK from the EU led to higher trade barriers, impediments to labor mobility, and lower capital flows, the TCA established new trade networks, boosting UK exports to the EU. At the same time, rising incomes and falling unemployment in the UK provided a spark to non-tradable production. The impact of these positive economic outcomes, in Period 3, was a higher level of GDP. A new period of economic expansion began.

Trade

During Period 1, both exports to the EU from the UK and imports into the UK from the EU increased on an annual basis, with the exception of

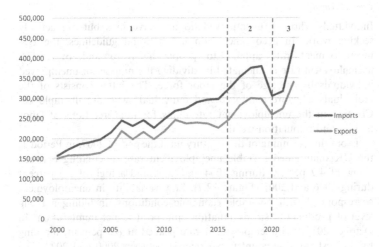

Figure 12.6 United Kingdom imports from and exports to the EU in current prices, £ millions.

Source: Author using data from the House of Commons Library, https://commonslibrary.parliament.uk/research-briefings/cbp-7851/.

the global financial crisis years of 2007 – 2008 and 2015 when exports declined over a one-year period and imports remained stagnant (Figure 12.6). These trends reflected a growing global economy and favorable trade conditions. Economic integration between the UK and the EU, US, and other parts of the world meant that the UK's exports and imports remained an important part of the economy.

In Period 2, the interim between the Brexit vote and TCA, both exports and imports rose. In 2019, the UK exported £298 billion worth of goods and services to the EU and imported £379 billion worth of goods and services from the EU. But, in 2020, a change occurred: exports declined to £258 billion and imports declined to £304 billion. The reason is that, from June 2016 to the end of 2019, expectations in the UK changed. After Brexit took place on January 31, 2020, uncertainty rose, leading to lower trade flows during 2020.

In Period 3, in addition to the implementation of the TCA, the coronavirus pandemic impacted trade. The novel coronavirus, disruptions in global production, and supply chain problems complicated trade flows. However, in 2021, the UK's exports and imports increased over their 2020 levels. By 2022, both exports and imports exceeded their 2019 levels, demonstrating stable trade conditions between the UK and EU.

Unemployment

Individuals who are unemployed do not have jobs but are actively seeking work. In accordance with international guidelines, the UK unemployment rate applies to people aged 16 and over. The **unemployment rate** is calculated by dividing the number of unemployed individuals by the size of the labor force. The latter consists of the individuals who are employed and individuals who are unemployed. Changes in the unemployment rate allow for interpretations of labor market and population trends.

From the beginning of this century until the end of 2007, in Period 1, the UK maintained a stable unemployment rate, fluctuating between a low of 4.7 percent during 2004 and 2005 and a high of 5.5 percent during 2006 and 2007 (Figure 12.7). Low variability in unemployment corresponded with favorable economic conditions, including a rising level of production, steady inflation, and positive net immigration. In October 2011, the unemployment rate peaked at 8.5 percent, marking the highest rate the country experienced between 2000 and 2022. The declining unemployment rate, which continued throughout the rest of Period 1, demonstrated that, after the global financial crisis, the UK's economy created employment opportunities.

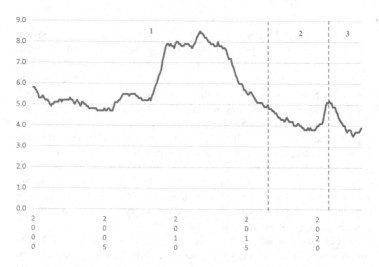

Figure 12.7 United Kingdom unemployment rate, aged 16 and over, seasonally adjusted, percentage.

Source: Author using data from the Office for National Statistics, https://www.ons.gov.uk/employmentandlabourmarket/peoplenotinwork/unemployment/timeseries/mgsx/lms.

After the Brexit vote, in June 2016, the unemployment rate continued to decline (Period 2). Between July 2016 and December 2019, the unemployment rate decreased from 5 percent to 3.9 percent, reflecting strong labor market conditions despite the Brexit vote. But, throughout 2020, the unemployment rate rose, reflecting the impact of the coronavirus pandemic, peaking at 5.2 percent in November 2020. During the pandemic, the UK government prioritized employment stability. The government advised businesses to maintain ties with their employees. As a result, the pandemic shock did not significantly increase the unemployment rate. To account for the decrease in economic activity, the government provided aid to workers.

In Period 3, the labor market improved. After January 2021, the unemployment rate declined, reaching a low of 3.7 percent in December 2022. One reason was a lower level of vacancies in the economy. Another reason was that older workers who left the labor market during the pandemic eventually returned. A rising level of payroll employment growth served as a final reason, as the economy began its post-pandemic phase while adjusting to its new trade position with the EU.

Key terms

Migrant
Peak
Sovereignty
Trough
Unemployment rate

Questions

1 What are the economic implications of Brexit?
2 What are the characteristics of the Trade and Cooperation Agreement?
3 How did Brexit impact the value of the British pound?
4 How did Brexit impact the flow of immigrants into the UK?
5 In the UK, did Brexit alter the rate of inflation? Explain.

References

Bryant, Ralph. 2018. "Brexit: Make Hard Choices but Don't Confuse Sovereignty with Autonomy." *Brookings*, December 21. https://www.brookings.edu/articles/brexit-make-hard-choices-but-dont-confuse-sovereignty-with-autonomy/
Castle, Stephen. 2023. "A Crab's Eye View of Brexit." *The New York Times*, April 7. https://www.nytimes.com/2023/04/07/world/europe/brexit-uk-seafood.html
De Lyon, Josh and Dhingra, Swati. 2019. "The Impact of the Brexit Vote on the Economy Is Now Clear." *London School of Economics*, March 23. https://

blogs.lse.ac.uk/businessreview/2019/03/23/the-impact-of-the-brexit-vote-on-the-economy-is-now-clear/

Dhingra, Swati and Sampson, Thomas. 2022. "Expecting Brexit." *Annual Review of Economics*, 14: 495–519.

Freeman, Rebecca, Manova, Kalina, Prayer, Thomas and Sampson, Thomas. 2022. "UK Trade in the Wake of Brexit." Discussion Paper 1847. Centre for Economic Performance, April. https://cep.lse.ac.uk/pubs/download/dp1847.pdf

Portes, Jonathan and Springford, John. 2023. "Early Impacts of the Post-Brexit Immigration System on the UK Labour Market." *Centre for European Reform*, January 17. https://www.cer.eu/sites/default/files/insight_JS_JP_17.1.23.pdf

Posen, Adam and Rengifo-Keller, Lucas. 2022. "Brexit Is Driving Inflation Higher in the UK than Its European Peers after Identical Supply Shocks." *Peterson Institute for International Economics*, May 24. https://www.piie.com/research/piie-charts/brexit-driving-inflation-higher-uk-its-european-peers-after-identical-supply#:~:text=We%20believe%20that%20Brexit%20is,of%20a%20simultaneous%20common%20shock

Tarr, William. 2022. "To What Extent Is Brexit Responsible for Britain's Excess Inflation?" *Harvard College Economics Review*, August 26. https://www.economicsreview.org/post/to-what-extent-is-brexit-responsible-for-britain-s-excess-inflation

Index

absolute advantage 28
Africa: population growth in 10; labor mobility in 55; climate disruptions in 89
aggregate demand 100–102
aggregate supply 100–102
Amazon Coins 72
American Rescue Plan Act 108
appreciation 74
arbitrage 77
Argentina: member of Mercosur 45, 51
arguments against free trade 30–31
ASEAN *see* Association of Southeast Asian Nations
Asia: value chains in 16; trade in 29; labor mobility in 55; pandemic in 110
Association of Southeast Asian Nations 45, 52

balance of payments 67
balance of trade 25
Belgium: original member of the EU 49; industrialization in 86
Belize: Gini coefficient in 92
Big Mac Index 82
Black Death 110
blockchain 71
Bolivia: member of Mercosur 51; economic development in 87
Brazil: emerging economy of 8; member of Mercosur 45, 51; Gini coefficient in 92; income classification in 113; foreign direct investment from 115; emerging economy characteristics in 116–117; oil production in 118

Bretton Woods 68–69
Brexit 9, 11, 49, 125
Brexit Uncertainty Index 125–126
British Central Bank 129
Bulgaria: labor mobility in 55

Cambodia: member of ASEAN
Canada: trade agreement in 50; international capital movements in 59; oil production in 118
carbon dioxide 87–88
Caribbean: trade in the 29
Central African Republic: Gini coefficient in 92
Chile: member of Mercosur 51
China: manufacturing and exporting in 2; entry into the World Trade Organization in 4; emerging economy of 8; global production network and 25; level of trade in 25; moving labor-intensive industries to 27; solar industry in 28; trade policy in 33–35; semiconductor production in 42; trade with Mercosur in 51; FDI in 62; production in services in 86; economic development in 87; carbon dioxide emissions in 89; emergence of the pandemic in 100; income classification in 113; foreign direct investment from 115; oil production in 118; emerging economy characteristics 120–122
choke points 17

climate change 2, 87
closed economies 25
CO_2 *see* carbon dioxide
Columbia: member of Mercosur 51
common market 47
comparative advantage 28
Consumer Price Index 108
consumer surplus 36–37
consumption effects 29
contagion 15, 110
convertible currency 69
COVID-19 100
cryptocurrency 71
customs union 47

deforestation 117
demand for foreign exchange 78
Denmark: trade of sugar cookies in 28;
    member of the EU 49
depreciation 74
developed country 6
developing country 6, 8, 86, 87
digital currency 71
diminishing marginal product of labor 57
distributional consequences 29

economic development 6, 85
economic inequality 91
economic integration 116
economic liberalization 113
economic linkages 62–63
economic sanctions 119
economic union 47
Ecuador: exporting bananas from 19;
    member of Mercosur 51
emerging economies 113
endogenous 99
England: trade in 28
environmental degradation 4
equilibrium 79
Eswatini: Gini coefficient in 92
Europe: value chains in 16; trade
    agreements in 18; beginning of
    World War II in 68; pandemic
    in 110
European Union: Brexit and the 9,
    125; migrants entering the 18;
    imports in the 18; trade
    agreement in the 44; regional
    trade agreement in the 48;
    labor mobility in the 54;
    currency values in the 70;
    unemployment in the 104

exchange rate 74
exchange rate volatility 75
exogenous 99
expectations 83

Facebook Credits 72
FDI *see* foreign direct investment
Federal Reserve Bank of New
    York 104
Federal Reserve System 20
Feenstra, R. 28
fiber optic cables 19
financial capital 2, 26
financial network 20
fiscal policy 108
floating exchange rates 66
foreign direct investment 61, 114
foreign exchange market 77
formal sector 89
forward transactions 78
fossil fuels 118
France: trading wine in 29; original
    member of the EU 49;
    industrialization in 86
Frankfurt: financial center in 77
free trade agreement 46
Fukuyama, F. 3

gains from trade 28
GDP *see* gross domestic product
gender gap 93
gender inequality 93
Germany: labor mobility in 55;
    industrialization in 86
globalization 1, 2, 4, 5, 18, 22, 110
global financial crisis 49
global production networks 24
global supply chain 104
Global Supply Chain Pressure
    Index 104
GNI *see* gross national income
gold standard 67
Great Britain: member of the EU 49
Greece: member of the EU 49
gross domestic product 9, 101
gross national income 5
GSCPI *see* Global Supply Chain
    Pressure Index
Guyana: member of Mercosur 51

IMF *see* International Monetary Fund
immigration 130
import quota 40

India: manufacturing and exporting in 2; emerging economy of 8; exporting rice from 19; global production network and 25; level of trade in 25; trading tea in 29; production in services in 86; income classification in 113; foreign direct investment from 115; emerging economy characteristics in 119–120
income classifications 5
Indonesia: member of ASEAN
inequality 4, 91, 92
infant industries 31
inflation 132
informal sector 89
institutional capital 115
international capital movements 59
international labor movements 55
International Monetary Fund 16, 62, 89, 123
international monetary system 66
Internet 17
Iran: oil production in 118
Iraq: oil production in 118
Ireland: member of the EU 49
Italy: original member of the EU 49; labor mobility in 55

Japan: exporting sushi from 19; solar industry in 28; trading automobiles in 29; semiconductor production in 42; international capital movements in 59; industrialization in 86

Keynes, J. 68
Kuwait: oil production in 118

labor force 119–120
labor market effects 30
labor mobility 54, 56, 58
Laos: member of ASEAN
level of trade 25
London: financial center in 77
Long Beach: shipping port in 18
long run 101
Los Angeles: shipping port in 18
Luxembourg: original member of the EU 49; FDI in 62

Maastricht Treaty 48
macro structures 16

Malaysia: member of ASEAN
marginal product of labor 56
Mercosur 45, 51
Mexico: manufacturing and exporting in 2; moving labor-intensive industries to 27; tourism and 74
microfinance 90
Microsoft Points
migrant 130
migration network 20; trade agreement in 50
MNEs *see* multinational enterprises
model of import demand and export supply 35–36
monetary policy 109
monetary union 48
Mozambique: Gini coefficient in 92
MPL *see* marginal product of labor
Multidimensional Poverty Index 94
multinational enterprises 114
Myanmar: member of ASEAN

NAFTA *see* North American Free Trade Agreement
Namibia: Gini coefficient in 92
Netherlands: trading cheese from the 29; original member of the EU 49; FDI in the 62
network 15, 18
New Jersey: shipping port in 18
New York: shipping port in 18; financial center in 77
Nigeria: population growth in 10
Nixon, R. 70
node 19
North America: value chains in 16; trade agreements in 18, 50
North American Free Trade Agreement 45, 50

OECD *see* Organization for Economic Cooperation and Development
open economies 25
Organization for Economic Cooperation and Development 134
Oxford University 94

Pakistan: population growth in 10
pandemic 4, 5, 8, 15, 17, 24, 25, 49, 65, 99, 102, 110

Paraguay: member of Mercosur 45, 51
peak 133
Peru: member of Mercosur 51
Philippines: member of ASEAN
Poland: labor mobility in 55
population 11
Portugal: trade in 28; member of the
    EU 49; labor mobility in 55
poverty 30, 93–94
PPP *see* purchasing power parity
preferential trading area 46
privatization 113
producer surplus 37–38
production function 55–56
production network 20
purchasing power parity 82

rate of return 79
regional trade agreements 5
regulatory mechanisms 17
Ricardo, D. 28
Romania: labor mobility in 55
Russia: conflict in 2, 119; emerging
    economy of 8;
    industrialization in 86; income
    classification in 113; foreign
    direct investment from 115;
    emerging economy
    characteristics in 118–119

Saudi Arabia: oil production in 118
Sao Tome and Principe: Gini
    coefficient in 92
scarcity 62
Scotland: fishing industry in 128
semiconductors 42–43
Shapiro, J. 29
shock 99, 126–127
short run 101
Silk Road 25
Singapore: member of ASEAN;
    financial center in 77
social network 21
sources of the gains from trade 28
South Africa: emerging economy of 8;
    Gini coefficient in 92; income
    classification in 114; foreign
    direct investment from 115;
    emerging economy
    characteristics in 122–123
South Korea: global production
    network and 25; importing
    financial capital in 26;

semiconductor production in
    42; international capital
    movements in 59; production
    in services in 86
sovereignty 126
Soviet Union 3, 5
Spain: member of the EU 49; labor
    mobility in 55; tourism in 74
special-purpose entities 62
spot transactions 78
subsidy 38
Suriname: member of Mercosur 51;
    Gini coefficient in 92
Switzerland: labor mobility in 55;
    industrialization in 86

Taiwan: semiconductor production
    in 42
tariff 38
TCA *see* Trade and Cooperation
    Agreement
technology and services hub 120
technology network 21
Thailand: member of ASEAN
Tokyo: financial center in 77
trade agreements 18, 44, 46–48
Trade and Cooperation Agreement 127
trade deficit 26
trade network 21
trade policies 38–41
trade surplus 26
trough 133
Trump, D. 45

Ukraine: conflict in 2, 4, 5, 17, 119
unemployment 104, 136
unemployment rate 136
uneven outcomes 22
United Arab Emirates: oil production
    in the 118
United Kingdom: population growth
    in the 9; level of trade in the
    25; withdrawal from the EU
    45; labor market shortage in
    the 55; FDI in the 62;
    exchange rate in the 66; gold
    standard in the 68; exports
    from the 75; interest rate in the
    79; supply of dollars in the 81;
    purchasing power parity in the
    82; industrialization in the 86;
    Brexit decision in the 125
United Nations 11, 94

United States: economic integration in the 2; exporting jobs from the 4; rising interest rates in the 4; population growth in the 9, 10; migrants entering the 18; level of trade in the 25; trade deficit in the 27; solar industry in the 28; trade of sugar cookies in the 28; trade policy in the 33–35; semiconductor production in the 42; trade agreement in the 50; international capital movements in the 59; FDI in the 62; gold standard in the 68; travel in the 69; imports into the 75; interest rate in the 79; purchasing power parity in the 82; industrialization in the 86; carbon dioxide emissions in the 89; unemployment in the 104; fiscal expansion in the 107–108; inflation in the 108; oil production in the 118; trade war with China in the 121–122

urbanization 4
Uruguay: member of Mercosur 45, 51
US-Mexico-Canada Agreement 45, 50

value added 90
value chains 16
vehicle currency 77
Venezuela: suspension from Mercosur 45, 51
vicious cycle of poverty 94–95
Vietnam: member of ASEAN
voluntary export restraint 40

White, H. 68
World Bank 3, 5, 9, 16, 17, 25, 65, 85
World Health Organization 110
World Trade Organization 4, 16, 17
World War I 68
World War II 16, 49
WTO *see* World Trade Organization

Zambia: Gini coefficient in 92

Printed in the United States
by Baker & Taylor Publisher Services